www.passthetexes.com

Pass the TExES

Pedagogy *and* Professional Responsibilities

FOR TEXAS TEACHERS.
A test prep manual for the TExES PPR
exam 160 for grades EC-12.

by Mark Mentze, M. Ed., M.A.
and Vickie Hester, Ph.D.

Fifth Edition

Pass the TExES PPR

Fifth Edition Copyright © October 29, 2018 by Ed Publishing and Consulting

Manufactured in the United States of America

≈

Published by

Ed Publishing and Consulting
888-978-1922
E-mail: edpublishing@passthetexes.com
Website: www.passthetexes.com

Writers/Editors: Mark J. Mentze, M.Ed., M.A.
and Vickie Hester, Ph.D.
Designer/Program Manager: Lori Mentze

PowerPoint® Study Module created by Lori Mentze

Designed using an Apple Macintosh iMac™ using Adobe's InDesign™. Fonts: Adobe Garamond, Bodega Sans, Matrix Tall, Wingdings. PowerPoint® is a registered trademark of Microsoft® Corp.

Dedication

To the late Helen Mentze who made my educational pursuits possible.

Contents

PowerPoint® study module instructions on the last page of this manual.

Preface

Dear Teachers:

This fifth edition of **Pass the TExES PPR** is a major expansion of our popular book. We think this is the best PPR test prep book available, and hope it is helpful to you as you prepare for the exam.

You may be planning to take the TExES exam shortly and are filled with apprehension like I was before my first certification test after moving to Texas several years ago. It is a scary thought to realize that if you can't pass the tests you could lose your job.

When I started to prepare for the old Professional Development ExCET exam (now the PPR) I was confused as to what I was supposed to study. I found a few resources, which I purchased and studied. However, I did not pass the first exam. For my second exam I used my graduate school study strategies. I gathered and abbreviated important information, outlined it, and created acronyms to help me memorize and recall information. I passed the exam the second time and raised my score by 13 points—a dramatic improvement. I also passed the TExES exam.

I expanded my materials so that other teachers could benefit from my study system. Illustrations, worksheets, new exercises, an interactive study module, etc., have been added. Our goal is to provide well-organized effective material for the PPR exam that is easy to study and internalize. **We really believe if you follow the instructions in the Steps for Success, (pp. 10-11) you will do well on the exam.**

Please note that at the back of this manual in the **Appendices** you will find **worksheets, the acronym tool, a Competency chart, our practice test worksheet, the seminar packet (includes duplicate worksheets)**, and important contact and resource information.

The information contained in this manual is useful to ALL TEACHERS who want to continue improving their professional skills, not just for passing the TExES exam. Learn it and apply it!

Pass the TExES seminars, tutoring, and additional content test preps for the TExES exams are available. See www.passthetexes.com or e-mail us at edpublishing@passthetexes.com

Good luck!

- Mark Mentze

Introduction

WHAT IS THE TEXES?
TExES stands for the Texas Examinations of Educator Standards. Legislation was passed in 1981 that mandates all public elementary and secondary teachers be tested and pass at least two certification tests. This book covers one of the two—many content exam test prep books are available from Ed Publishing at www.passthetexes.com.

WHERE CAN I REGISTER FOR THE TEXES?
Registration information is found at www.tx.nesinc.com. Important contact information:

TExES Program for Texas Teachers
Pearson Education
www.tx.nesinc.com
800-989-8532

or the SBEC (State Board
for Teacher Certification):

SBEC
1701 North Congress Ave.
WBT 5-100
Austin, TX 78701-1494
Phone: 888-863-5880
or 888-863-5880
www.tea.texas.gov

CHARACTERISTICS OF THE EXAM
The TExES program is designed to assess subject matter knowledge and professional knowledge required of an entry-level educator in Texas public schools. All the exams in the TExES program are criterion referenced; that is, they are designed to measure your knowledge in relation to an established competence (criterion) rather than in relation to the performance of other candidates.

HOW SHOULD I STUDY FOR THE EXAM?
Of course you should obtain the study manual provided by NES/SBEC (see www.tx.nesinc.com). In the back of the manual several reference books are listed which would be helpful to review if you have time, and will likely be available at your local university or community college library. However, time is most likely limited, so we encourage you to use this book in conjunction with the study manual provided by the NES/SBEC, and you will have a complete test preparation package. There are other publishers who have produced TExES study manuals and in them you may find additional sample test questions...however, use our approach for preparing for the exam and answering practice test questions. You can view a list of those alternate resources in Appendix II of this manual. **It is very important to follow the Steps for Success in this manual.**

WHEN ARE THE EXAMS GIVEN, AND HOW MUCH DO THEY COST?
The exams are give at locations throughout Texas. All the information you need regarding test dates, site locations, fees, registration procedures, and policies can be found at www.tx.nesinc.com, where you can also register online.

This program is designed to help you understand all the Competencies and their important concepts in the shortest amount of time possible. If you successfully complete the work in this program you will likely pass the test. We have received hundreds of testimonials over the past several years from teachers who have enjoyed using our material and who have passed their tests successfully.

NOTE: Tests are no fun, but a benefit to taking these TExES tests is that the information is very valuable to teachers. The better you know the study material, and the more you apply it, the better teacher you will be.

Introduction, cont'd.

EXPLAIN THE PASS THE TEXES PROGRAM...WHY DO I NEED IT?

This study program is designed in such a way to make preparing for the exam more efficient for the learner, and more effective. The program is all about TOOLS. We give you several tools which will help you prepare for the exam like no other program. The exercises presented in our program encourage methods of study that will help you retain more information in a shorter amount of time. The program exercises were designed to naturally strengthen the analysis and synthesis skills of the learner, which is key when choosing the best answers to the test questions. Our program addresses several learning styles and preferences.

WHAT ARE THE FEATURES OF THE PROGRAM?

Of course it is essential to be knowledgeable about the subject matter, but these tests consist of many subjective questions. To help you organize the material we have created some tools that are very helpful. The ACRONYM EXERCISE in Appendix I is designed to help you recall the COMPETENCY KEY TITLES (see Competency 1's KEY TITLE at the top of p. 15); the KEY TITLES are designed to recall the COMPETENCY study material, and with the help of the KEY WORDS (see p. 14), the content for each Competency should be recalled more efficiently.

The official NES/SBEC TExES study manual contains bulleted descriptive statements for each Competency. The KEY DESCRIPTOR exercise described in the Steps for Success, p. 10, (and in each Competency study section) asks you to condense these descriptive statements into short phrases which require you to analyze and synthesize the NES/SBEC descriptive statements instead of just passively reading them. The PRACTICE TEST METHOD explained in Appendix I will help you choose the BEST answer to the exam questions. There is also a PRACTICE TEST WORKSHEET and PRACTICE QUESTIONS in Appendix III in this manual. Please follow the directions on the Practice Test Method page in Appendix I to answer these questions and any other practice test questions available from various sources.

The WORKSHEETS in Appendix I are very important, and help you understand the framework of the material. You may copy these pages and complete them multiple times to test your recall.

The PowerPoint® interactive STUDY MODULE is the icing on the cake. The module is another way to study the framework of the content. It breaks down the Competency definitions into phrasing for better understanding. See instructions for use on the last page in this manual. *(NEW! Online TExES Ebook Modules (TEMs) are also available.)*

TWO KEYS TO THIS PROGRAM

 INTERNALIZING IMPORTANT CONCEPTS FOR EACH COMPETENCY.

 UNDERSTANDING HOW TO CONNECT TEST QUESTIONS TO THE CORRECT COMPETENCY AND CHOOSING ANSWERS BASED UPON THE SBEC POINT OF VIEW.

GOOD LUCK! After you receive your score, send your success stories and comments to edpublishing@passthetexes.com. We would love to hear from you. Visit www.passthetexes.com and read the many testimonials we have received about the program.

Steps for Success

. . . .

NOTE: It is recommended that 3-4 weeks is allowed to complete this study program process. There are certain exercises that you may not have time for. However, choose the parts of the program that you feel you can realistically accomplish, set some goals, and plot them on a calendar.

1 STEP ONE (ACTIVE STUDY)

a. To begin your test preparation you will need the **state's NES/SBEC official study** manual. The manual is available online at http://www.tx.nesinc.com, and we have included the study material from the manual in Appendix III of this book. (NOTE: If you feel you need additional study, there are recommended resources listed in the back the NES/SBEC manual.)

b. We call the bulleted study information in the NES/SBEC manual **"Descriptors"**. This is key conceptual information, although the statements are sometimes difficult to understand and study because of their length and wordiness. The author's study material in this manual is an expansion of these Descriptors. Our "Descriptor Exercise" below will help you understand the Competency concepts more clearly and will help strengthen your analysis skills, skills you will need on the actual test.

c. **Review the author's study material for the first Competency in this manual.** Study the Key Title, Descriptor Highlights, Key Words and chapter content. Use your highlighter to highlight key information, and use the Internet to quickly look up information you need further clarification about and write additional notes in the margins. NOTE: If you are using an ebook you can highlight right in the PDF file.

EXAMPLE:

"Knows the typical stages of cognitive, social, physical, and emotional development of students in early childhood through grade 12."

The paraphrase for this bullet point is "<u>stages of development</u>"

Taken from bullet 1, Comp. 1, PPR EC-12

d. **Descriptor Exercise:** *Use the official SBEC study material in the back of this book for this exercise.*

Before you move on to Competency 2, do the Descriptor Exercise for Competency 1. This exercise is a great tool to help you understand what the SBEC wants you to know, and will help you retain that information more efficiently and more effectively. Study and analyze the bulleted descriptive statements under each Competency definition in the NES/SBEC manual (not just passively read them), and synthesize them down to a phrase that is meaningful to you and that will concisely sum up what the bullet point is stating. (See the example at left.) On the blanks on p. 14 record your phrases and keep your phrases at **six words or less**; put one phrase on each blank. It is helpful to number the bullet points and blanks. Then transfer all of your phrases to Worksheet 4 in Appendix I of this manual for easier study.

2 STEP TWO (MEMORIZATION)

The Descriptor Exercise is designed to not only help you understand with the SBEC wants you to know, but helps you commit information to memory. When you read your phrases, you will hopefully be able to recall additional details. In the example the important information that we left out was the stages of development: "cognitive, social, physical, and emotional". This is what you will hopefully recall when you read the phrase "stages of development". A good way to study with Worksheet 4 is to put it beside the SBEC study material and go back and forth, checking your recall of additional details about the Competency concepts.

a. Study the Acronym page in Appendix I before you do Worksheets 1-3. It is necessary to continue studying while you are attempting to complete these worksheets over time. The goal of Worksheets 1-3 is to organize and internalize the framework of the state material. *TIP: When you are on the actual test, sometimes stress and fatigue can make it difficult to recall details from your study unless you have the framework in mind.*

b. Worksheet 5: A few assignments to do after you have spent time studying all of the content.

c. Use the PowerPoint® Study Module as an alternate fun exercise to check your memory of the framework of the material, and to assist you in understanding the Competency definitions. The definitions are broken down into shorter phrases, "who, what, how, and why" to make them easier to understand.

  WE RECOMMEND: On the test booklet before the test write down your acronym (see Appendix I), then your Key Titles. As you answer each question, if needed, refer to this Competency framework to refresh you memory about what you learned in your study of each Competency.

Steps for Success, cont'd

3

STEP THREE (ASSESSMENT)
Go to the Practice Test Worksheet and Practice Question Section in Appendix III. Also, go to the PRACTICE TEST METHOD page in Appendix I. On this page we explain how to use the Practice Test Worksheet in detail. The seven italicized questions on the Worksheet represent a very methodical thought process of analysis of questions. By following this method carefully while working each question, you will better connect the test question to the Competencies which is key to choosing the best answer, and you will understand the point of view of the SBEC, which is very important to your success. Choosing correct answers based on incorrect reasoning only sets you up for failure. In the seventh step of this process, you are analyzing for yourself why the test writers chose the answers they did, and that is KEY, especially on the more subjective questions. *TIP: Doing this analysis will help you understand the philosophy of the test writers, as well as strengthen your analysis skills...skills you will need on the actual test.*

THE OVERALL APPROACH

The overall approach you are following when using the Pass the TExES study program of study is in two parts:

Part One: Knowledge and Comprehension

Part Two: Critical Thinking Skill Development

According to Bloom's Taxonomy knowledge and comprehension material must be mastered before one can apply these concepts in the test questions. The Pass the TExES program encourages the development of higher level thought processes such as application, evaluation, and analysis and synthesis...processes Bloom's Taxonomy categorizes at the top end of learning. The exercises we employ are designed to exercise and increase these higher-level thought processes, thus allowing for greater success on the exam. That is why this method includes both lower level memorization activities and then moves into exercises using the higher level thought processes. The goal, of course, is to know this material well and be able to analyze test questions and choose correct answers on the test.

★ **This program has made all the difference for many teachers since 1999. Read testimonials and purchase additional copies of this book and other books at www.passthetexes.com. Seminars may be available to the general public and they are always available for Texas universities, school districts, Alternative Certification Programs, and Education Service Centers.**

NOTE: By carefully following this program of study we feel that you will be well-prepared for your TExES exam. However, we do not guarantee a passing grade on the exam. We encourage you to contact us during your study time should you have any questions. If you purchase a book and decide you cannot use it, please contact us within one week of receipt to request a refund. We're sorry, but there are no refunds on ebooks.

Domain I:

Designing Instruction and Assessment to Promote Student Learning

Competencies 1-4

(31% of the test)

Pedagogy and Professional Responsibilities Standard I:

The teacher designs instruction appropriate for all students that reflect an understanding of relevant content and is based on continuous and appr opriate assessment.

1. Human Development

Key Descriptors:

_____

_____

_____

_____

_____

_____

_____

_____

_____

_____

_____

_____

_____

_____

_____

Key Words:
Cognitive, Social, Physical, and Emotional Development

Variations

Impact of Delays Across Domains

Signs of Delays

Stages of Play

Life Skills

NOTE: Refer to the bullet points under each Competency in the NES/SBEC study guide. Analyze each bullet point, and synthesize it down to a paraphrase that is meaningful to you, using no more than 5-6 words. List those phrases in order on the lines above. It may help to number the bullet points and the lines above. When complete, record them again on Worksheet 4 in Appendix I.

DESCRIPTOR HIGHLIGHTS

- Knows the stages of cognitive, social, physical, and emotional development (the four domains).
- Recognizes that variations occur.
- Uses development to plan instruction and assessment.
- Selects developmentally appropriate instructional activities.
- Analyzes how developmental delays in one of the four domains affects other domains.
- Recognizes signs of impairment or delay.
- Knows the importance and stages of play.
- Teaches life skills.
- Recognizes challenges for each developmental stage.
- Understands the importance of peer relationships.

1. Human Development

. . . .

Competency 1:

The teacher understands human development processes and applies this knowledge to plan instruction and ongoing assessment that motivate students and are responsive to their developmental characteristics and needs.

The State of Texas expects all teachers to analyze their individual learners. We are not teaching a subject or a grade—we are teaching individual students. Each student arrives with a unique history and experience set that has led to his/her current growth and mindset. By analyzing where students are in their development, teachers can plan effective, personalized instruction that allows all learners to progress. There are four main developmental domains:

- Cognitive (thought, thinking)
- Social (relationships, morality)
- Physical (body, brain)
- Emotional (feelings)

A. Cognitive Development

Cognitive development involves the growth of thinking skills and processes. The primary educational researcher in this field was Jean Piaget, whose studies described interactions between learners and their environments. He categorized these interactions in stages. The first three stages are typical for PK-4th grade. The fourth stage develops at varying rates, but typically at around 5th-6th grade.

Paiget's Stages (SPCF)
S - Sensorimotor
- Generally occurs ages at 0-2.
- The child explores the world using their senses (everything goes into the mouth, etc.).

- Listening occurs from birth; speech develops toward the end of the first year.
- The child is extremely attached to primary caregiver.
- Object Permanence is a common trait for this stage (out of sight, out of mind). This impacts learning as items out of sight cease to exist in the child's mind, which can lead to anxiety (especially over "lost" parents, "lost" home, etc.).

P - Preoperational
- Generally occurs at ages 2-7.
- The child engages in imaginative play, using symbolic items and familiar roles.
- The child's thinking is more advanced, but still not based on logic.
- Egocentric: "it's all about me" - The child does not grasp that others have different ideas and perspectives than they do.
- The concept of conservation is not fully developed.

continued

Teachers need a basic understanding of human development: physical, mental, emotional and social. People act in certain ways to shape and form their environment. There is a constant interaction between people and their environments.

---

1. Human Development

Conservation - A specific quantity (particularly of liquid) will remain the same despite the size, shape, or dimension of the container it is in

Child sees these as having the same amount when the concept of conservation is fully developed.

4 ounces in each container

This means the child has moved from the preoperational stage of thought to the concrete stage of thought.

C - Concrete
- Generally occurs at ages 7-11.
- The child demonstrates higher-order, more logical thought.
- The child still engages in exploratory learning, but learning is thought-driven as opposed to driven by senses.
- Fully understands conservation.
- Knowledge is assimilated by *doing* (active, cooperative learning is appropriate - project based learning, discussion groups, etc.).
- Understands relational terms, that things can have predictable relationships, can categorize.
- Understands *reversibility*, that things can be done, then undone.

F - Formal
- Generally occurs ages at 11 and up.
- Higher thought, creation, evaluation, and synthesis.
- Self-directed (student-centered) learning is most appropriate.
- Child is able to research, debate, justify, defend, and extend his/her own learning.

Sample Question: A preschooler has a pitcher of milk. After pouring milk from the pitcher into three cups, the preschooler announces that she now has more milk. The teacher's best assessment of this incident would be that the student:

a. appears to be showing signs of a developmental delay.
b. has not grasped the concept of conservation of volume.
c. appears to be showing signs of a visual disability.
d. has not developed the concept of object permanence.

Cognitive Development and Impact on Language Development

Students who have limited experiences with books and print at home may need several years of development of experiences related to print awareness at school. These students' ability to connect through oral language, to develop reading skills and phonemic awareness (as well as to understand information presented in these ways) is negatively impacted. Students will ultimately be less successful in life if the concepts are not developed at an early age.

Implication: We need to fill in the gaps for these students and provide the missing experiences.

Students who have interacted with significantly older individuals in their home environment will develop mentally from the interaction. They will have:
- Enhanced thinking and reasoning skills.
- Higher vocabulary skills.

Implication: We need to allow these advanced students to progress while filling in the gaps for students who lacked these experiences.

Wide exposure to reading is an excellent method to reach both groups.

B. Social Development
Moral Development - Based on Kohlberg's Stages of Moral Development
Note that stages are not necessarily tied to a specific age, but do progress chronologically. Moving to the next stage is dependent on the child's cognitive

1. Human Development

ability to perform at that level. For example, an adult with severe developmental delays may perform in the self-interest orientation stage.

Kohlberg's Stages of Moral Development

1	2	3	4	5	6
Obedience and Punishment Orientation	Self-Interest Orientation	Conformity Orientation	Social Order Orientation	Social Contract Orientation	Universal Ethical Principles

Pre-Conventional Children	Conventional Adolescents	Post-Conventional Adults

Level 1 (Pre-Conventional)
Most common in children

1. Obedience and Punishment Orientation -
    Whether or not to do something is dir ectly related to the consequence. Will I get in trouble? Can I avoid punishment?

2. Self-Interest Orientation -
    Focus is on satisfying own needs...an egotistical attitude. Works for rewards, but may not work if no apparent reward is offered. Extrinsically motivated. What's in it for me?

Level 2 (Conventional)
Most common in adolescents

3. Conformity Orientation -
    Focus is on pleasing others, per forming as expected, "being good".

4. Social Order Orientation -
    Focus is on following rules and laws to maintain society's expectations. Law and order mentality.

Level 3
(Post-Conventional)
Most common in adults

5. Social Contract Orientation -
    Focus is on doing what's allowed vs. what is right. Laws and rules can be bent (or disregarded) for the

good of the whole. Personal values guide decisions and realization is present that values vary from person to person. Example: Driving five miles over the speed limit.

6. Universal Ethical Principles -
    Behavior and morality is guided by personal principles of right and wrong...an individual's perception of what matters most. Right choices ar e made simply because they are right, without recognition or reward, regardless of consequence. Some adults never attain this level of moral growth.

C. Physical Development
Environmental Factors and Prenatal Development
During prenatal development, negative occurrences can have impacts that affect development throughout a child's life. Specific considerations are:
*   Maternal nutrition
*   Malnutrition linked to increased risk of birth complications, neurological problems, and psychopathology
*   Maternal drug use
*   Tobacco, alcohol, prescription, and recreational drugs
*   Fetal alcohol syndrome
*   Maternal illness:
    Rubella, syphilis, mumps, genital herpes, AIDS, and severe influenza can affect development
*   Prenatal health care

Teachers should be aware that when these situations are present, the child may have delays that will impact all domains. Guidance from health and education professionals is associated with higher success rates in students with developmental needs.

D. Emotional Development
Early Emotional Development
*   Attachment - emotional bonds are formed between child and caregiver(s)
*   Separation anxiety - emotional distress occurs when the child is separated from caregiver(s)

continued

1. Human Development

Emotional Development is Affected by Parenting Styles
- Authoritarian - strict and punitive; no reasoning with children
- Permissive - little restrictions or control
- Authoritative - has rules, but reasons with children
- Uninvolved - shows little interest; at extreme is neglectful (abuse)

Personality Development - Based on Erik Erikson's Stages of Personality Development
The following stages illustrate the importance of a positive school experience since school is usually one of the main places where children are separated from their parents.

Stage One
Trust vs. Mistrust
0-1.5 years
- Parental attachment and control is very important for the child's sense of trust to develop.
- During this stage, the child's needs must be met in order to move to the next stage.
- Babies feel greater sense of attachment (mistrust) when needs are not being met (clingy, whiney).

Stage Two
Autonomy vs. Doubt
1.5-3 years
- During this stage, the child begins to develop a sense of control over him/herself. The child develops self-confidence in newly found independence.
- He/she feels doubt, shame, and guilt when parents are too controlling or overprotective.

Stage Three
Initiative vs. Guilt
3-6 years
- During this stage, the child may feel guilty if parents are too attached or controlling.
- The child begins to assert him/herself and initiates activities.
- The child learns to control him/herself according to the norms of the given situation and he/she learns to do what is expected.

- It is important not to encourage guilt for small misdeeds at this stage.

Stage Four
Industry vs. Inferiority
6-12 years
- The child begins to develop a sense of success or failure for accomplishing certain tasks (very important in school).
- At this stage, children set goals for themselves and tries to reach them.
- Social interaction becomes more important to the child.
- Children want to become more independent and parents and schools need to encourage this independence.

Stage Five
Identity vs. Confusion
12-18 years
- The child begins to develop a sense of personal identity.
- Begins to focus on future goals and pathways.
- Strives to create a unique persona, and sometimes rebels against societal norms.

E. **Variations**
Individual differences are caused by various factors:
- General intelligence
- Physical development (eyes, ears, gross and fine motor skills)
- World experiences and schemata (things they've seen and done)
- Home environment and enrichment, parental education, etc.
- School experiences and how child is treated at school
- Interaction with adults and older individuals

Developmental differences can occur in different areas, such as physical growth patterns, cognitive development, moral development, personality development, social and emotional development.

1. Human Development

In short, no two children are alike. Growth happens in predictable stages, but not to everyone at the same age or time reference.

F. Planning Instruction and Assessment

Teachers need to assess students' stage of personality development

- to be aware of developmental delays
- to modify activities as necessary to meet the needs of all learners
- to respond appropriately to students' develop mental stages
- to plan lessons and activities that foster growth for each child.

When planning for appropriate instruction, a teacher should:
Assess all students and their developmental stages in all areas -

- Physical
- Cognitive
- Personality
- Morality

Plan activities to meet deficiency needs.
Examples:
• *A child with a lack of self-esteem*
Teacher gives the child a special classroom job, such as feeding the class pet.
• *A child with a visual perception deficiency.*
Teacher provides material on a sheet of paper, as well as writing it on the board.

Plan activities to meet the needs of advanced students.
Examples:

- Give students a choice of extension activities or enrichment activities.
- Allow students to design their own learning experiences by beginning special projects.
- Provide advanced materials.
- Implement instruction that provides a variety of stimuli—visual, auditory, kinesthetic.

G. Delays and Impacts Across Domains

Factors that affect the physical growth and health impacts their development in other domains (e.g., cognitive, social, emotional):

- Vision - developed through early childhood. Vision deficits affect learning because children are conditioned to respond to visual patterns, objects, events, and people around them.

- Perception - developed by the child's conditioning to respond to various stimuli within the environment.

- Bone Development - takes place as a child's bones are growing and developing, gradually hardening. Bones are resilient but severe blows can result in permanent physical damage, which may cause problems with fine and gross motor skills.

- Balance and motion (both linear and rotary) are developed through normal activity, but vary greatly from child to child.

- Brain cells grow by the 100 billions during pregnancy and are developed throughout childhood by stimuli from visual, auditory, and emotional sources of information. Experiences cause brain development to vary between children.

- Health factors, such as ear infections in early childhood, may affect the child's ability to learn language and linguistic processes. Mild or moderate hearing loss, even a temporary loss, may affect development. Signs to watch out for: not paying attention, saying "huh?" when spoken to, not following directions, withdrawing from peers, being overactive or uncooperative.

H. Recognizing Issues

Experiences in early childhood affect development throughout the child's school experiences. As children learn and develop skills—or fail to develop skills—their future is impacted. Because of this, early identification of needs is imperative. *continued*

1. Human Development

Indicators of Developmental Deficits:
- Lack of social skills
- Cannot keep up with routine tasks and the demands of school life
- Developmental delay
- Behavior abnormalities (irritation, hyperactivity, withdrawal, violence)
- Disorganization and inability to cope with classification tasks
- Focusing problems
- Abnormal facial development
- Shorter finger length
- Jitteriness
- Abnormal development of oral cavities (can lead to speech problems, hearing and visual problems, inattentiveness, over-activity, comprehension problems)

Stages of Cognitive Development - Red Flags:
- Student does not speak
- Student is excessively attached to caregiver
- Student does not engage in play
- Student older than five rejects all peer interaction

Stages of Cognitive Development - Normal:
- Student prefers to play with only one kind of toy
- Student chooses toys that are associated with opposite gender (i.e., boy who wants to dress up in princess costume)
- Student who cries when separated from parents (except when crying for extended period, i.e., days and weeks)
- Student prefers to play with only one or two friends

I.   Stages of Play
Play is an important and necessary part of learning. It is the entire "job" of a child. During play, children build:
- oral language skills
- thinking skills
- the ability to solve problems
- memory
- the ability to plan and anticipate the future
- investigative skills that are critical for self-directed learning

- organization skills
- understanding of societal expectations and roles
- social skills that relate to all parts of life

Types of Play:

Solitary Play
A child is in a room full of other children, but is playing alone and not paying attention to anyone.
- Playing with blocks alone

Parallel Play
Playing next to each other with the same game or toy, but they are not talking or doing the same activity.
- Playing in the block area, but one student is building towers and another is connecting linking blocks

Associative (Onlooker) Play
Watching other children and talking with peers may seem passive but they are very alert to the action around them.
- Watching other children who are putting puzzles together at the table

Cooperative Play
Playing effectively and cooperatively with peers
- Playing a board game, taking turns
- Serving dinner to friends in the dramatic play center

J.   Life Skills
Teachers must incorporate activities that foster student growth in these vital areas:
- Self-direction
- Decision-making
- Goal-setting
- Organization
- Workplace skills

K. Challenges
Teachers must be aware of these challenges that children face and must develop lessons and activities that are sensitive to these issues:
- Self-esteem

1. Human Development

• •

- Physical appearance
- Peer relationships
- Eating disorders
- Identity formation
- Educational and career decisions
- Risky behaviors
- Social and emotional factors in the family (divorce, homelessness, etc.)

L. Peer Relationships and Classroom Environment
Teachers should understand the importance of peer relationships, and should develop activities that foster positive peer interactions. Factors for consideration:

- Importance of peers
- Peer acceptance
- Conformity to peer norms
- Peer-related issues for teaching and learning

2. Diversity

Key Descriptors:

_____

_____

_____

_____

_____

_____

_____

_____

_____

_____

_____

_____

_____

_____

_____

_____

NOTE: Refer to the bullet points under each Competency in the NES/SBEC study guide. Analyze each bullet point, and synthesize it down to a paraphrase that is meaningful to you, using no more than 5-6 words. List those phrases in order on the lines above. It may help to number the bullet points and the lines above. When complete, record them again on Worksheet 4 in Appendix I.

Key Words:
Ethnicity, Culture
Language Differences
Gender
Disabilities
Exceptionality
Multicultural Awareness
Student Interests
Socioeconomic Diversity
Equity

Hands-On Projects for Kinesthetic Learners

DESCRIPTOR HIGHLIGHTS

- Understands student diversity (ethnicity, language, gender) and uses this knowledge to plan instruction and assessment.
- Accepts, learns about, teaches respect for other cultures.
- Uses diversity to enrich learning setting.
- Adapts lessons for English language learners (ELLs), students with disabilities, and gifted students.
- Adapts lessons to provide equal access to tools and opportunities for success for all students.
- Is sensitive to providing equal access to technology.
- Understands students' learning needs and preferences.

2. Diversity

• •

Competency 2:

The teacher understands student diversity and knows how to plan learning experiences and design assessments that are responsive to differences among students and that promote all students' learning.

When we think of diversity (differences), our minds tend to automatically jump to the consideration of ethnicities. Ethnicity is only one of many ways that students are different. Respect for student diversity requires teachers to consider:

- Ethnicity
- Culture (beliefs, behaviors and traditions of their family/heritage)
- Language strengths and needs (ELLs)
- Gender
- Home life and background experiences
- Financial situation as related to access to materials for study, research and projects
- Access to technology
- Cognitive differences, particularly for students with delays and students who are gifted
- Developmental differences
- Learning styles (visual, auditory, kinesthetic)
- Student interests and preferences

A. Ethnicity and Culture

With each passing year, the state of Texas becomes more ethnically and culturally diverse. Understanding of diversity is a necessity for success in teaching and learning. As technology blooms, the workplace of tomorrow is globally connected. In many companies, work teams connect through the Internet, while the workers themselves live in many countries and represent many nationalities. For this reason, we must also teach our students to value and respect cultures—to help them build bright futures without boundaries.

- Ethnicity - the common physical characteristics that define a group of people (i.e., "race") —Hispanic, Native American, African American, Anglo American, etc.

- Culture - the common behavioral characteristics that define a group of people—traditions, beliefs, religion, language, holidays, food, clothing styles, etc.

Our purpose as teachers, ultimately, is to prepare students for success in college and the workforce. Students that embrace the diversity of others have more success—and more opportunities. Because diversity is so critical, many questions on the TExES test contains elements of, or focus on, this Competency.

B. Language

More than 140 languages are represented in Texas schools. More than two million English language learners (ELLs) fill our schools. Understanding of the special needs of English language learners will help teachers assure success for all students.

1. Developmental Stages of Language Acquisition
Students develop skills with second languages in predictable patterns. Evaluating where the student is along the language acquisition path helps teachers plan instruction that reaches the ELL.

a. Home language - student uses their home language only, and only communicates with others who speak this language. At this stage, it is helpful to pair the students with partners who are fluent in both the home language and in English.

b. Silent period - student does not participate and speaks very seldom, even in their home language. At this stage, the student is listening and absorbing language, making mental connections between the new language and their home

continued

2. Diversity

● ●

language (translating in his/her mind). This complicated task is consuming most of the student's mental energy. It is a mistake to think the student is "slow" or "not paying attention" at this predictable stage.

c. Formulaic Speech - student speaks like a caveman or infant, in one or two word statements that represent a need. For example, "Water". The teacher must interpret whether this means the student wants water, there's been a spill, etc. At this stage, the student will benefit from learning more words in English and you should provide help toward vocabulary acquisition (dual language dictionaries, labels in both English and home language, peer help, bilingual books, etc.).

d. Social Language - student can converse about everyday things, can ask for things he/she needs, and is easily mistaken as fully fluent. Student still needs vocabulary building assistance.

e. Academic Language - student can read and understand second language, including academic and abstract concepts (such as metamorphosis, freedom, similes, idioms, etc.)

NOTE: To build second language skills, student need to talk. Provide frequent opportunities for students to converse and discuss relevant material, ideas, and concepts.

2. ELLs and the Law
Providing accommodations for ELLs is a legal requirement. Teachers cannot require the use of English-only in their classroom, and cannot deny or belittle any home language or culture. Teachers should be versed in the TEKS and the law regarding ELLs.

TEKS:
http://www.tea.state.tx.us/index2.aspx?id=6148
Law: http://ritter.tea.state.tx.us/rules/tac/chapter089/ch089bb.html

3. Evaluation for ELLs
To accurately assess ELLs, teachers should:
* Use a variety of assessments, including written, oral, and performance measures.
* Allow students multiple opportunities to demonstrate their learning.

4. Support for ELLs
* Provide assistance where needed (peer helper, extra time to complete assignments, help from you, bilingual texts when appropriate, alternate assessments and assignments, reduced written assignments, etc.)
* Connect with colleagues (the ESL teacher, school specialists, etc.) who may have insight or materials to help. (Remember to respect student confidentiality. More information on this is located in Competency 13.)
* Know the law and the TEKS for ELLs, and adhere to these guidelines.
* Frequently check for student comprehension of assignments, material, and expectations.
* Garner support and help from family members to reinforce concepts the student is learning by supporting lessons at home (discussing materials and lessons in the student's home language, visiting museums and libraries, reading books on the topics studied, etc.).
* Increase your own knowledge and skills regarding helping ELLs (staff development, book studies, research, etc.)

NOTE: All learners should learn all objectives. Never dumb-down the lesson or leave out parts because this hurts the student. Find other ways to get there, but everyone should end up at the goal!

C. Gender
Though commonly used in schools, gender grouping is not a best teaching practice. Students must learn to work with others, regardless of gender.

Heterogeneous grouping—mixed groups, some boys and some girls—are the state expectation for classrooms.

2. Diversity

D. Home Life and Background Experiences; Equitable Access to Tools, Materials, and Technology

Learning begins at home. Students come to us with a variety of background situations. Sensitivity to the child's home life allows teachers to recognize when a student needs support or lacks background experiences (schemata) necessary to understand new concepts. Common situations in test questions:

- Student has low self-esteem - provide opportunities for the child to gain feelings of success (special helper, classroom job, etc.)
- Student's home life is chaotic - provide extra structure for the child and predictable expectations
- Student lacks materials or financial resources to get materials - provide opportunities for the child to complete the task using supplied materials, allow the child to choose an alternate project, have the child work collaboratively with others on a joint project
- Student lacks background to understand a concept being presented - build the background by explaining, demonstrating, or showing pictures
- Student lacks technology or technology background - provide access to technology while at school and partner the child with other students who know how to use the equipment but require student to participate at all stages. Provide technology that can be checked out and used at home.

E. Deficit (Struggling) Learners

Every student has strengths and weaknesses. Do not label students who struggle, but instead realize these students have strengths in other areas. Supports for deficit learners:

- Assess/build upon prior knowledge
- Build background
- Preview unfamiliar concepts/words before the lesson
- Use visuals
- Relate to previous lessons and concepts learned
- Review as needed

- Use cooperative learning strategies
- Partner more able students with those having difficulty
- Modify activity/assignments based on teacher observation/ELL checklist/Individual Education Plan (IEP), including reduced written assignments, use of larger tools (chunky crayons, my first pencil, gripper scissors) and pre-cut pieces, and scribing assistance.

NOTE - Modifying assignments does not mean reducing the learning expectations. All learners should master all objectives.

- Provide individual teacher assistance
- Provide frequent opportunities for review/re-teaching/revisiting concepts learned previously
- Continually observe/monitor students
- Restate and repeat instructions
- Demonstrate activity
- Provide tutoring

Be certain to follow student's Individual Education Plan (I.E.P.) if one is in place. This is the law— failure to follow an I.E.P. is breaking the law and prosecutable.

F. Gifted Learners

Gifted learners are the innovators of tomorrow. Their bright minds are in constant motion, and they have their own ideas and beliefs. They tend to be perfectionists and if they cannot or are not allowed to complete projects in the way they envision, these children become frustrated. Gifted learners must be allowed choice and the opportunity to extend the learning in their own, unique way. If teachers fail to allow exceptional students to use their gifts, they tend to shut down and do little or nothing. Ways to help gifted students:

- Partner them with students who are able to keep up with them. Do not make them teacher helpers or partner them with low-performing children. (This frustrates both children.)

continued

2. Diversity

• •

- Provide them choices—choices of projects, choices of materials, choices to design their own learning experience.
- Allow them to "chase rabbits" - explore side interests sparked by the learning.
- Give them opportunities to extend their learning —Internet research, games, projects.
- Collaborate with the school's gifted student specialist.

G. Learning Styles

Each has a learning style—a way he or she learns best. The most common learning styles are visual, auditory, and kinesthetic. Excellent lessons present material in all three ways. This way each learner gets the material in the way he/she learns best, and has it supported in two other ways.

• Visual learners learn best by being shown. Demonstrations, models, and step-by-step instructions are very helpful to visual learners. Visual learners also thrive on pictures, graphs, charts, diagrams, and technology-based presentations (movies, PowerPoint® presentations, slide shows, etc.).

• Auditory learners absorb information by listening. They seem to have a mental sound recorder — once they've heard something, they tend to remember it. Auditory learners do well with short lectures, explanations, discussions, and technology-based presentations. They also do well with recorded books, music-based learning, and whenever soft music is played in the background.

• Kinesthetic learners file information in their mental filing cabinet when they are moving. (Kinesthetic means movement.) These bright students are often wrongly categorized as "hyper" or "behavior challenges", when really, they simply cannot learn without movement. When we stop them from moving, we might stop the learning. Best practices for kinesthetic learners include teaching them non-disruptive movements, being observant of their needs and offering movement opportunities in the classroom, and

incorporating hands-on activities into lessons.

H. Student Interests and Preferences

When students are interested in a topic, they drive their own learning and frequently accomplish far more than adults expect. For this reason, the state wants teachers to utilize student interests to inspire motivated learning.

Examples:

- Students learning about adjectives could describe characters in a popular movie.
- Students learning about social studies could compare a social hero to a comic book hero.
- Teachers can use student discussions of current events to introduce lessons or concepts.
- Teachers should take advantage of "teachable moments"—those opportunities that occur and may be off-topic, but offer opportunity for learning. (Example: The students notice butterflies outside. The teacher chould use this moment to discuss the metamorphisis of butterflies.)

Students should be given choice of project and should drive their own instruction. (Would you like to make a poster, a model, or a comic strip? Would you like to write a diary entry, a story, or an interview? What is most important for us to learn about this?)

I. The Bottom Line

Two truths:

- You are not teaching science, math, or English. You are not teaching 3rd grade or 5th grade or seniors. You are teaching children. Individual children. Students are unique...and you must teach—and reach—every one of them.
- Children aren't problems. Children have problems. If you can diagnose the problem and treat it, the problem will likely go away. Look past the problem and find its root. Look past the problem and see the child.

2. Diversity

J. Teaching Multicultural Awareness and Respect for Diversity

The goal of multicultural awareness is that students will understand, value, and respect different cultures and people who are different than themselves. Human nature is to draw together based on similarities. Even adults group themselves with others whose culture, beliefs, and ideas match their own. However, in the work- force, we must be able to get along with others despite differences, lest we fail. To teach students to value and appreciated differences, we should:

- Allow students to work with others who are different (in a variety of ways) from themselves
- Explore other cultures
- Discuss the characteristics that make each culture and person unique and special
- Compare others to ourselves and find commonalities—ways in which we are similar and can therefore connect
- Teach tolerance

Never divide students by similarities. It robs students of the opportunity to develop these necessary skills.

K. Other Expectations

In addition to teaching students to respect diversity, teachers must continually build their own understanding of others. This can be accomplished by:

- Staff development
- Classes and advanced education at a college or university
- Personal research and study
- Book and/or journal study
- Reflecting on your performance and looking for personal bias
- Collaborating with others to build skills

L. The TExES Test: Wrong Answer Choices

- Anything that separates students by similarities (gender grouping, ability grouping, grouping by ethnicities)
- Anything that punishes students for their diversity or for failing to accept the diversity of others (this builds more resentment instead of appreciation)
- Anything that ignores the diversity of students (and thereby fails to meet their needs)
- Anything that only addresses the needs of the majority (teaching to the middle level students, ignoring language differences because most of the students can understand, etc.)

3. TEKS

Key Descriptors:

_____
_____
_____
_____
_____
_____
_____
_____
_____
_____
_____
_____
_____
_____

NOTE: Refer to the bullet points under each Competency in the NES/SBEC study guide. Analyze each bullet point, and synthesize it down to a paraphrase that is meaningful to you, using no more than 5-6 words. List those phrases in order on the lines above. It may help to number the bullet points and the lines above. When complete, record them again on Worksheet 4 in Appendix I.

Math Teacher

Science Teacher

Project Planning

Key Words:

Texas Essential Knowledge and Skills
  (TEKS)

Learning Goals

Prior Knowledge

State Assessments

Resources from Outside the School

Developmentally Appropriate Activities

Logical Lesson Progression

DESCRIPTOR HIGHLIGHTS

- Understands the TEKS, their purpose and form.
- Evaluates learning goals for clarity, relevance, significance, age-appropriateness, ability to be assessed, meets the students' needs, meets district/campus goals.
- Uses assessment to see what students need and to evaluate teacher effectiveness.
- Understands how TEKS and state assessments work together.
- Uses state assessment data to plan instruction that meets the students' needs.
- Evaluates and uses technology resources and resources from other sources to engage (motivate) students.
- Uses developmentally appropriate learning activities.
- Designs lessons that move systematically and logically so that concepts build upon each other and are understandable.
- Allows students to explore content from many different points of view (perspectives).
- Makes time for lesson closure, lets students reflect and evaluate their learning.

3. TEKS

Competency 3:

The teacher understands procedures for designing effective and coherent instruction and assessment based on appropriate learning goals and objectives.

A. The TEKS

The State of Texas has developed a vertically and horizontally aligned, standards-driven curriculum to promote cumulative knowledge and skills.

- Vertically aligned - knowledge builds from grade to grade. Students gain a concept in one grade, and expand their knowledge in the next.

- Horizontally aligned - knowledge and expectations travel from subject to subject. For example, students should be writing in English language arts, math, science, and social studies.

Linking subject areas provides meaningful learning experiences that develop skills and knowledge, while leading to an understanding of conceptual relationships. With integrated curriculum, skills and knowledge are developed and applied in more than one area of study. Multiple links can be made among the language arts, mathematics, humanities, communication arts, natural sciences, social studies, music, and art.

Texas teachers must have comprehensive knowledge of the Texas Essential Knowledge and Skills (TEKS), and must use this knowledge to plan, implement, and assess effective instruction. The TEKS provide clear goals that both teachers and students can understand, assess, and achieve.

It is advisable to spend time exploring the TEKS prior to taking the TExES (especially content area) exams. The TEKS can be downloaded from: http://www.tea.state.tx.us/index2.aspx?id=6148

B. Evaluating Learning Goals

Learning goals are the driving force behind education. All lesson objectives require careful consideration. Test each objective for:

- Clarity - Is what your students will be learning clear?
- Relevance - Is what your students will be learning relevant to their lives?
- Significance - Is what your students will be learning important? Does it represent the big ideas?
- Age-Appropriateness - Is the work you have planned right for the age group?
  - Remember, young children (EC-2) have limited attention span and a great need to be moving. A long, written assignment would be inappropriate.
  - Older children (2-5) can perform concrete operations and can readily do paper and pencil tasks.
  - Mature children (grades 6 and up) are capable of detailed, abstract thought. They should spend time evaluating and directing their learning.
- Ability To Be Assessed - Are your goals measurable? All objectives should be designed so learning can be measured by a finite action or product.
  - For example, "The student will know..." or "The student will learn..." are poor objectives because you cannot finitely measure these things.
  - Better objectives are "The student will explain...", "The student will explore..." or "The student will perform..."
- Responsiveness to Students' Current Skills and Knowledge, Background, Needs, and Interests - Do your students have the prerequisite knowledge to accomplish your objec-

continued

3. TEKS

tives? Do you need to build background knowledge before your objectives can be effective? Have your students already mastered these objectives? How can you tie your objectives to your students' interests? Are there special needs you should address? Remember, you are teaching students, not curriculum. Adapt your lessons to where your students are and they will be more successful.

- Alignment with District and Campus Goals - You work for a "company"—your district—at your campus. Your company has set goals based on the needs of the student population at your campus. Your lessons should marry themselves to the TEKS first and foremost, but should also be aligned with your district and campus goals.

C. Using Assessment
In the school setting, both students and teachers tend to hate assessment and to view it as a form of punishment. Assessment is not meant to be negative—instead it is a valuable tool for both the teacher and the learner. Assessment tells students what they know and what they need to learn. Assessment tells teachers how effective their lessons and demonstrations have been, and about the specific needs of each student.

Types of Assessment
- Formal - These are traditional tests, usually multiple choice, essay, etc. They may be measured based on specific criteria (criterion-referenced) or may be based on how the group as a whole performs (norm-referenced).
- Informal - These are daily scores, teacher observations, portfolios, journals, class work, answers to questions, etc.
- Formative - Formative assessments are tests and observations that are given as concepts are being taught (forming)
- Summative - Summative assessments are given at the end (sum) of units, semesters, courses, etc.

The annual state assessment is a formal, summative assessment.

What Assessment Is
- A tool to measure and drive learning and instruction
- A tool for teachers and learners
- A measurement of what students know
- A measurement of how effective lessons have been
- A chance for children to shine—to show how smart they are becoming
- A state expectation and requirement
- Important!

What Assessment Is Not
- A time filler
- A punishment
- A measurement of who or what a learner is
- A measurement of how smart a learner is
- Optional

How to Use Assessment
Assessment should be used to:
- See how well students are progressing
- Identify learning gaps and needs
- Identify where students lack background experiences that are necessary for understanding
- Reflect upon your lessons and performance
- Design instruction that meets your learners' needs

D. How the TEKS Relate to State Assessments
The TEKS and the state assessments go hand-in-hand. The assessment measures the students' learning of the TEKS. The assessment mirrors the TEKS in such a way that the state can assess teacher performance based on how well students perform on the test. There are mitigating factors that play into student performance, but as a general rule, if a teacher teaches the TEKS, the students should perform well on the annual state assessments.

3. TEKS

E. Making Data-Driven Decisions

The primary reason for assessment is to allow the teacher to analyze students' strengths and needs. Teachers should use assessment data to plan activities and lessons that meet the needs of the individual learners in their classrooms.

F. Evaluating Resources

Because guest speakers, materials from outside sources (newspapers, magazines, museum enrichment materials, etc.), and technology resources (Web sites, PowerPoint presentations, videos, etc.) are highly motivating to students, these materials should be used to enrich your lessons. Effective teachers must:

- Evaluate the materials and their content
- Determine if materials are appropriate for students
- Be sure materials are age-appropriate
- Make sure materials align with the TEKS, your campus and district goals, and your lessons

G. Selecting Developmentally Appropriate Activities

Young children (EC-2) have a limited attention span. The best lesson activities include:

- Short periods of discussion
- Active games and activities that allow movement
- Activities that encourage development of both fine and gross motor skills
- Singing, dancing, dramatic play
- Short review of basic skills
- Read alouds
- Fun!

Older children (2-5) can perform concrete operations and can readily do paper and pencil tasks. The best lesson activities include:

- Short periods of student-driven discussion
- Cooperative learning, group activities and discussion
- Projects and project-based learning
- Student-directed learning - students have many choices and a say in how they learn and are assessed; students make decisions about their work and how they will demonstrate their learning; students evaluate their own performance and coach their peers; students do the work (answer choices that have the teacher doing the work are wrong!)
- Technology components - video, audio, computer-based
- Short review of basic skills (no worksheets)
- Read alouds
- Independent reading
- Fun!

Mature children (grades 6 and up) are capable of detailed, abstract thought. They should spend time evaluating and directing their learning. The best lesson activities include:

- Student-driven discussion at a high level, about relevant and abstract concepts
- Cooperative learning, group activities and discussion
- Projects and project-based learning
- Student-directed learning - students have many choices and a say in how they learn and are assessed; students make decisions about their work and how they will demonstrate their learning; students evaluate their own performance and coach their peers; students do the work (TExES test answer choices that have the teacher doing all the work would be incorrect.)
- Technology components - video, audio, computer-based
- Independent research and learning
- College and career readiness, life skills instruction
- Independent reading for increasingly longer periods
- Read alouds
- Fun!

continued

Notes

3. TEKS

● ●

H. Logical Lesson Progression

Lessons and units should progress in an orderly way so that skills build upon previously learned skills. Instruction should be student-centered, engaging, and active. Lesson progression steps:

1. Gain attention - use a "hook" to get students interested in what they will learn.
2. Activate prior knowledge—elicit information students already know about the topic.
3. Use graphic organizers to map developing awareness of concepts, prior knowledge, predictions, purpose for learning (What do you want to know? Why is this important?).
4. Teach the concepts in an active way (technology, discovery, maps, guest speaker, etc.).
5. Present new knowledge clearly in a step-by-step fashion. Include relationships between previous concepts and future concepts.
6. Discuss and use informal assessment all along the way to be sure students are gaining the desired knowledge.
7. Demonstrate how to perform any tasks you are requiring.
8. Have students help you complete a couple of examples.
9. After the concepts are fully formed, have students use what they know and create their own projects or complete the task on their own.

Circulate and offer help and support (scaffolding) as needed.
10. Close the lesson. Have students evaluate and discuss what they learned, how it fits into their overall knowledge core, and why it is important.
11. Assess student learning.
12. Re-teach concepts as needed.

I. Selecting Correct Answers

• Remember, the TEKS are law. They should guide all lesson objectives.
• Assessment is important. Do not devalue or avoid assessment.
• The most accurate picture of what a student knows is formed by a variety of assessments. Use several types of assessment to obtain valid information.
• Assessment data should drive your instruction. Use this data to make lessons that assure all children are successful.
• The use of technology, outside resources, and presenters is a state expectation. This is for the students' benefit.
• The right answers center on the needs of our students. Remember, it's all about the student!
• The best teachers are evaluative. Use assessment to improve your personal teaching skills.

4. How Learning Occurs

Key Descriptors:

_____

_____

_____

_____

_____

_____

_____

_____

_____

_____

_____

_____

_____

_____

_____

NOTE: Refer to the bullet points under each Competency in the NES/SBEC study guide. Analyze each bullet point, and synthesize it down to a paraphrase that is meaningful to you, using no more than 5-6 words. List those phrases in order on the lines above. It may help to number the bullet points and the lines above. When complete, record them again on Worksheet 4 in Appendix I.

Key Words:

Instructional Strategies

Developmental Differences and Needs

Range of Thinking Abilities

Critical Thinking

Higher-Order Thinking Skills

Organizational and Time Management Skills

Graphic Organizers

Cooperative Learning

Self-Directed Learning

Project-Based Learning

Teacher/Student Roles

Acronym List for the TExES Test Material

1. H
2. D
3. T
4. H
5. E
6. M
7. C
8. E
9. T
10. A
11. F
12. P
13. T

DESCRIPTOR HIGHLIGHTS

- Understands how learning occurs.
- Connects new learning to prior knowledge.
- Makes learning meaningful and relevant to students.
- Plans lessons for young children that use movement, sensory input, and direct experiences.
- Understands that middle years are transitional and students show a range of development.
- Works with older students on skills and attitudes, including commitment to stay in school, skills for getting along with others, appreciation for diversity.
- Recognizes how the characteristics of students at different developmental levels impact learning.
- Uses understanding of the range of thinking abilities exhibited by students in any grade level.

- Teaches students to reflect, think, and analyze.
- Builds higher-order thinking and inquiry skills.
- Teaches organization and time management.
- Teaches study skills.
- Teaches effective research skills.
- Analyzes teacher behaviors that impact learning with a focus on eliminating negative behaviors.
- Analyzes ways home and community factors affect learning.
- Uses self-directed learning strategies to enhance student motivation.
- Analyzes teacher and student roles and how these impact learning.
- Teaches lessons that meet the learning styles of all students (visual, auditory, kinesthetic).

4. How Learning Occurs

Competency 4:

The teacher understands learning processes and factors that impact student learning and demonstrates this knowledge by planning effective, engaging instruction and appropriate assessments.

A. How Learning Occurs

The Old Way of Teaching:

In classrooms of yesterday, the teacher stood at the front of the class and lectured. Students dutifully took notes and sat in long, silent rows. Engagement was low. Behavior, not learning, was rewarded. Many concepts were learned, but not mastered. Over time, concepts learned but not mastered had slipped away.

Today's Classrooms:

Classrooms of today are animated and noisy. The teacher stands before the class for only a brief time, and then facilitates discussion and activities. Students drive the learning, questioning, debating, and discussing. The focus is on teamwork and active learning. The teacher's job is to facilitate— to assure that learning is occurring and objectives are being met.

The Learning Pyramid

The National Training Laboratories' Learning Pyramid demonstrates that students learn more by active, hands-on lessons.

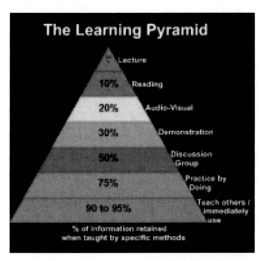

Adapted from original research by the National Training Laboratories, Bethel, Maine

Though there is some debate about the authenticity of this research and its numbers, teaching practice shows that students retain the most information when all of the sections of the pyramid are included in lessons. In other words, students should hear a small amount of lecture, read some about the concepts they are learning, see some visuals, etc. The bulk of instruction should focus on hands-on activities, projects, and discussion. As a culmination, students should present and justify their work.

Words To Know

• *Schema/Schemata* - Schema is simply an experience from the past that one can use to relate to new information. The word "schemata" is the plural form of schema. When students lack schemata (background experiences necessary for understanding), teachers must build this background. For example, if a student has never seen snow, they may need to see some pictures of a snow-covered house before they can understand how story characters feel when they peer out over the snow and are homebound because of it.

• *Scaffolding* - Scaffolding in the construction world involves building a frame or structure to support a wall until it is strong enough to stand on its own. In the teaching world, scaffolding serves the same purpose—it is a help or support put into place to support learners until they can stand on their own. In short, scaffolding is help. Some types of scaffolding are:

• Teacher or peer assistance
• Flashcards
• A multiplication chart
• Tutoring
• A peer helper
• Teacher notes
• Graphic organizers
• Bilingual books

continued

4. How Learning Occurs

● ●

B. The Importance of Activating Prior Knowledge

The key that opens the door of knowledge is experience in the world. Children draw meaning from experiences based on their unique ways of thinking, their interests, and their prior knowledge.

To help students gain understanding of new content, teachers must connect lessons to a child's present and past experiences, prior knowledge, and interests.

C. Knowledge Background

Students must have sufficient background knowledge to assimilate new content. Imagine taking an advanced calculus class without first studying basic calculus. Students feel completely lost when considering higher-level concepts without prerequisite learning. When students do not possess knowledge background, there is missing scaffolding for the new material. Assessing and building students' background knowledge increases student comprehension. These steps are critical instructional measures to ensure that all students are able to connect new learning to their prior knowledge and experience.

D. Activating Prior Knowledge and Relevance

Students learn and remember new information best when it is linked to relevant prior knowledge. Teachers who link classroom activities and instruction to prior knowledge build on their students' familiarity with a topic and enable students to connect the curriculum content to their own culture and experience. Teachers can activate prior knowledge by:

- Leading class discussion
- Using graphic organizers that activate and illustrate students' prior knowledge

This graphic organizer has students fill out what they know and what they want to know about a specific topic prior to study. After the lesson cycle is complete, they can cement their learning by filling out the last column, what they learned.

Example: The KWL Chart

Topic: Japan		
K What I Know	**W** What I Want to Know	**L** What I Learned

Such dialoging and visualizations also encourage students to think about their thinking (What do I do in a particular situation and why?), transferring the thought processes to a conscious level.

By tapping their students' prior knowledge in all subject areas, teachers can plan lessons that will:

- Clarify incomplete or erroneous prior knowledge
- Determine the extent of instruction necessary in a particular topic area
- Discern necessary adjustments to planned independent activities and assessment materials
- Use prior knowledge to make instruction more meaningful
- Help students understand and appreciate the experiences and contributions of people from different backgrounds

E. Making Learning Meaningful and Relevant

Teachers must engage students in meaningful activities that incorporate prior learning and are relevant to their lives. Teachers must use a wide variety of learning activities that:

- Reflect the students' cultural diversity
- Reach the students' learning styles
- Make sense
- Have real-world applications
- Connect to prior knowledge

4. How Learning Occurs

● ●

In making learning meaningful, teachers should take advantage of teachable moments—moments when the students come in with their own concerns, information about current events, or questions regarding things they have observed in their world.

F. Teaching Young Children

How Learning Occurs for Young Children
Young students are egocentric, concrete thinkers who gain information primarily through sensory input. The best lessons for young children will:

- Be concrete (use manipulatives or real-world exploration)
- Have sensory input (have elements that appeal to the five senses)
- Be active (developing both fine and gross motor skills)
- Involve direct experiences

G. Teaching Older Students

A Transitional Stage
Older students and adolescents are making a transition from childhood to adulthood. Their search for identity often takes precedence over their academic pursuits. In addition to academic concepts, students need to develop:

- Interpersonal skills
- An appreciation for diversity
- A commitment to stay in school

H. How Developmental Levels Impact Learning

Development impacts learning in all stages. For younger children, questions focus on:

- Attention span
- Need for activity and movement

For older children and adolescents, questions focus on:

- Importance of peers
- Search for identity
- Questioning values
- Career and life goals

I. Teaching to a Range of Thinking Abilities

In any classroom, teachers will have students with a mix of developmental ranges. To begin, teachers need to analyze and identify their students' developmental levels. Then, this information should be used to plan lessons that reach the students' needs. For example, in a middle school classroom where some students are still in the Concrete level of development, the teacher should plan some activities that are hands-on, use manipulatives, and have visuals, as these will meet the developmental needs of the low-level students, while still engaging those who have attained the Formal level of development.

The Power of Grouping
One effective method for helping students with a mix of thinking abilities and developmental levels is to pair them effectively. The best pairings are flexible—groups change based on interest and activity. A good rule is to pair:

- Low - Medium
- Medium - High
- High - High

NOTE: Never teach to the middle, leave out lesson parts, or dumb-down the lesson. All learners master all objectives.

J. Teaching Students to Think, Analyze, and Reflect

To be successful, teachers must:

- Understand the importance of play
- Use manipulatives
- Encourage students to create and test hypotheses
- Engage in problem solving activities
  - Hands-on
  - Challenging
  - Structured

Create an Environment of Exploratory Learning
Create a Learning Community - where learning, questioning, researching, and discussion are fostered

continued

4. How Learning Occurs

K. Inquiry-Based Learning

Inquiry-based learning is a style of teaching in which children drive the learning process based on questions that they generate. Teachers become coaches, guides, and facilitators who help learners arrive at the important questions—the things they really care about. When students choose the questions, they are motivated to learn and they develop a sense of ownership about the project.

Advantages:

- Students learn to identify and refine essential questions
- They learn to seek out information for themselves as opposed to awaiting input from others in a passive manner. These skills are critical for future success.
- Inquiry-based learning is flexible and easily adapts to meet the needs of individual learners.
- Inquiry-based learning is highly engaging.
- Inquiry-based learning is well suited for collaboration.
- It works with students of any age.

L. Higher Order Thinking Skills

Developing higher order thinking skills for our students is an important part of learning. These skills originate with Benjamin Bloom's Taxonomy. There is more about Bloom's Taxonomy in Competency 7.

M. Other Important Skills We Must Teach

To be successful, students today require complex skills. We have much more than content to share with our students. In addition to standard curriculum, teachers must also teach:

- Organization and time management skills
- Study skills
- Research skills

N. Teacher Behaviors

Many teacher behaviors influence how learning occurs within the classroom. We must:

- Demonstrate appropriate, high expectations
- Have positive interactions with students and parents
- Use effective grouping strategies

O. Home and Community Factors

In planning learning experiences, teachers must be aware of the role played by:

- Parent expectations
- Community resources
- Community problems

P. Self-Directed Learning

Self-directed learning occurs when students actively seek new learning. This happens when teachers allow the students input on their lessons. Students develop ownership of their learning—and go above and beyond our expectations—when we step out of the way and allow them a measure of choice. Students should have some choice regarding:

- How information is obtained
- What tools they will use
- How they will demonstrate their learning
- Some of the criteria by which they will be assessed
- What project(s) they will do
- Who they will work with as partners

Even though we act as facilitators for learning, we must:

- Establish the learning objectives
- Help the students craft projects that lead to the objectives being met
- Work with students to be certain we met our objectives

Q. Learning Styles

See this section in Competency 2.

4. How Learning Occurs

R. The TExES Test: Selecting Correct Answers

- If the teacher is doing the majority of the work, it is less likely to be correct than options in which the students are doing the majority of the activity or work.

- Note that routines and procedures are important. Teachers must teach these explicitly because they safeguard learning time, provide structure for students, and teach students to organize, a necessary life skill.

- For younger kids, choose the more active options, particularly for PK-1.

- Don't be the boss, be the facilitator.

- Higher on Bloom's Taxonomy is better.

Domain II:

Creating a Positive, Productive Classroom Environment

Competencies 5-6

(15% of the test)

Pedagogy and Professional Responsibilities Standard II:
The teacher creates a classroom environment of respect and rapport that fosters a positive climate for learning, equity and excellence.

5. Environment of Support

Key Descriptors:

_____

_____

_____

_____

_____

_____

_____

_____

_____

_____

_____

_____

_____

_____

Key Words:

Classroom Environment

Collaborate

Respect

Supportive Interactions

Active Engagement

High Expectations

Room Arrangements

Safe, Nurturing Environment

Modeling

NOTE: Refer to the bullet points under each Competency in the NES/SBEC study guide. Analyze each bullet point, and synthesize it down to a paraphrase that is meaningful to you, using no more than 5-6 words. List those phrases in order on the lines above. It may help to number the bullet points and the lines above. When complete, record them again on Worksheet 4 in Appendix I.

DESCRIPTOR HIGHLIGHTS

- Uses developmental knowledge to create a positive environment.
- Teaches sharing and cooperation skills to young children.
- Teaches older children to collaborate with peers and to treat the community with respect.
- Emphasizes collaboration and support.
- Teaches respect for diversity.
- Creates an environment where students are actively engaged.

- Analyzes teacher-student interactions and student-student interactions with a focus on eliminating negative interactions.
- Shows personal enthusiasm for learning.
- Conveys high expectations.
- Arranges room to support safety, productivity, accessibility, and learning.
- Creates a safe, nurturing environment for all students.

5. Environment of Support

Competency 5:

The teacher knows how to establish a classroom climate that fosters learning, equity, and excellence and uses this knowledge to create a physical and emotional environment that is safe and productive.

A. Development and Classroom Climate

Children develop in stages (see Competency 1), and with these stages come unique needs. Before entering the school setting, many students have little or no experience working and playing with others, particularly with others who represent diverse characteristics. In building a positive classroom climate, teachers must consider the developmental stages represented within their classrooms.

At the beginning of school, you can set the stage for a positive classroom by leading a discussion on how we want to be treated by others. Guide the students to develop their own guidelines of what should happen within their learning community. Have students agree together to follow their guidelines. Also discuss how infractions can be handled in a positive manner (ask him/her to stop, move away, tell the teacher), and when they should be immediately brought to your attention (when there is an injury or hazard).

B. What Younger Children Need

Younger children do not arrive with skills that, as adults, we take for granted. Children in these early stages are very egocentric. They have a difficult time comprehending that what is best for them is not best for everyone.

Children do not innately know how to do these important tasks:
- Share
- Take turns
- Move past each other
- Use words instead of actions to accomplish goals
- How to be polite

- How to respect the possessions of others
- How to be honest and fair

Teachers must teach young learners these skills:
- How to work together, take turns, and share
- How to treat others and how to respect diversity
- Friendship skills
- Line behavior, cafeteria behavior, audience behavior
- How to ask for things instead of grabbing or pushing
- How to ask for help
- How to behave when one has accidentally hurt or wronged someone
- How to become a self-manager—to control one's own behavior and to make right choices

Important aspects of teaching these skills:
- Explaining and demonstrating expectations
- Consistency
- Modeling professional behavior

C. What Older Children Need

Older children are able to comprehend matters that are increasingly abstract. Their peer association skills should be centered on success in their future lives. Middle level students should have many opportunities for group interaction. Older students must be taught to respect their community and the people within. They need explicit instruction regarding:
- Skills for life
- Collaboration
- Respectful interactions
- Interpersonal skills
- Decision-making skills

continued

5. Environment of Support

D. Creating a Collaborative Environment
- Physical space - classrooms should be arranged in ways that support collaboration and provide clear passage between spaces
- Emotional space - students should be taught to respect the feelings and emotions of others
- Respectful interactions - students must learn to demonstrate respect for diversity and to interact in ways that demonstrate respect for themselves, others, and their learning community
- Organize for success - an organized environment allows smooth transitions between activities

E. Teaching Respect for Others
Respect is an attitude that will carry children far in life. Without respect for others (and for authority), children will have many challenges as they grow. There are many ways to teach respect.
- Model respect. Children who are shown respect understand how important respect is.
- Discuss respect. Children should understand that respect means how you treat others, how you treat their possessions, and how you treat yourself.
- Work with parents. Make parents your partners in teaching and modeling respect.

Specific ways to respect diversity
- Find common ground
- Explore and value uniqueness
- Share personal information and become friends

F. Keeping Students Engaged
Engagement is interest. When students are engaged, they participate enthusiastically and learn more.

Why Engagement Is Important
The opposite of engagement is boredom - which often leads to misbehavior. Keep your students challenged and excited about what they are learning and behavior challenges vanish.

How Engaged Learners Look and Act
Engaged learning is noisy. Enthusiasm bubbles as students relate what they are learning to their personal experiences. Engaged learners are animated, often out of their seats, leaning forward, and waving their hands in the air to comment.

How Disengaged Learners Look and Act
The old adage, "Idle hands are the devil's playground", is very true. Disengaged students talk about irrelevant things, appear bored, counter the teacher, clown for attention, and disrupt the learning of others.

How To Foster Engagement
Students are most engaged when
- lessons are appropriate and comprehensible
- lessons are meaningful and relevant
- work and expectations are clear
- there are active components to the lesson
- they are given choices and input into their learning

Specific Ways to Foster Engagement
- Create lessons with active and interactive components.
- Provide clear expectations and goals, preferably set with the help of the children.
- Offer choices of materials, projects, and methods of assessment.
- Allow students to work together.
- Use real-world examples.
- Design lessons that use student interests.
- Use technology (videos, audio, projectors, computers, overhead, visuals, presenters, slide shows, learning games, etc.).

G. Interactions
Teacher-student interactions can build or destroy your classroom climate.

- Praise and correct behaviors, not children. When you single out a child—for correction or praise—it can have an effect on the child and the classroom. Public criticism may cause children to escalate behaviors to save face. Public praise may also make children the target of harassment and jealousy. It is

5. Environment of Support

● ●

important to praise and correct students, but strive to do so privately.

• Redirect and prevent student misbehaviors before they escalate. Focus on the expectation (what you want students to do as opposed to what you want them to not do) and remind the group as a whole of your expectations.

• Get personal while remaining professional. Let students come to know you as a person. Share photos of your pets, talk about your hobbies, and discuss the books you are reading. Admit your failures, and own your feelings. Likewise, care about their personal interests. Notice their new shoes, ask about their sports team, and ask them to share about what they are reading. This builds relationships. When you have a relationship with a student, they will exceed your expectations. An important note: maintain boundaries with your students. For instance, do not exchange personal contact information.

• Motivate students. Motivate students by making learning fun, by making your classroom a place they want to be, and by creating a climate where they know they are valued and respected.

H. What the Teacher Should Model
Children watch you and learn from everything you do. Because of this, the state expectation is that teachers will:
• Model respect for colleagues, parents, authority figures, and the community
• Demonstrate respectful care for the property of others (especially school and district property)
• Model a love of learning
• Convey high expectations—that all students can and will successfully master all objectives
• Demonstrate positive problem-solving skills

I. Room Arrangements
Classrooms should be arranged to allow collaboration, accessibility, and smooth transitions. Safety is also paramount.

The Old Way
• Students in straight rows facing the front.
• Teacher often sits at desk in the front and stands in front of the chalkboard/whiteboard.
• Little or no technology in use.

The Classroom of Today
• Students sit at tables or in desks arranged for collaboration.
• Teacher desk is not front and center in the classroom.
• Many types of technology in use.

Effective Arrangements
Many arrangements can be used, but the most effective arrangements allow the students to work cooperatively and independently with little or no furniture movement. The most common desk arrangements are:
• Tables (Four desks pushed together, or actual tables.)
• Clusters (Several desks pushed into a configuration that allows shared work.)
• The "U" (Desks form a U shape, facing inward and toward the instructional area.)

Using the Periphery
The area around the periphery, or the edges of the room, can be used for centers, classroom library, and displays. Centers should be arranged for easy movement and independent use.

Organization Tips from Veteran Teachers:
• Post your respect agreement.
• Get along with your colleagues and the students' parents. Never let a child see you showing disrespect—verbally or non-verbally. Don't complain in front of the students.
• Keep crayons and basic supplies in baskets on the tables.
• Avoid having students at the sink. Keep pre-moistened towels for table clean-up.
• Do not allow students to throw or break supplies. If they do, require a replacement.

continued

Notes

5. Environment of Support

- Use large box lids for storing paper.
- Have students bring a plastic shoebox with lid to store their projects and tools. These stack nicely and are airtight.

J. **The TExES Test: Selecting Right Answers**

The following answer choices are not correct:
- Anything that isolates a child
- Anything that draws negative attention to a child
- Public praise or correction
- Room arrangements that do not allow accessibility or collaboration
- Punishing children harshly, especially for questioning you
- Showing bias, favorites
- Grouping by similarities

- Boring lessons, particularly those that have the students as listeners and observers instead of as active participants
- Lessons that do not allow collaboration
- Anything that fails to respect diversity or to teach the children to do so

6. Management Issues

Key Descriptors:

_____

_____

_____

_____

_____

_____

_____

_____

_____

_____

_____

_____

_____

_____

NOTE: Refer to the bullet points under each Competency in the NES/SBEC study guide. Analyze each bullet point, and synthesize it down to a paraphrase that is meaningful to you, using no more than 5-6 words. List those phrases in order on the lines above. It may help to number the bullet points and the lines above. When complete, record them again on Worksheet 4 in Appendix I.

Key Words:

Routines and Procedures

Collaborative Skills and Activities

Balanced Schedule

Transitions

Technology

Paraprofessionals and Volunteers

Behavior Management

Ethical Behavior

Behavior Management

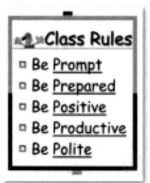

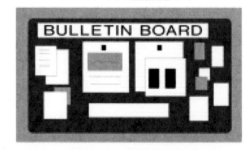

D E S C R I P T O R   H I G H L I G H T S

- Creates age-appropriate routines and procedures.
- Understands how development and age affect collaborative skills.
- Teaches children to work together cooperatively.
- Creates effective schedules that balance restful activities, active movement activities, play, projects, and centers.
- Manages time, materials, transitions, and balances non-instructional activities with instructional activities.
- Uses technology for administrative tasks.
- Works effectively with volunteers and teacher assistants.
- Applies behavior management techniques
- Understands behavioral expectations for different age groups.
- Uses procedures for behavior management with a focus on promoting positive behavior.

6. Management Issues

Competency 6:
The teacher understands strategies for creating an organized and productive learning environment and for managing student behavior.

A. Some Important Words To Know
Collaboration - working in small groups, or teams

Cooperative Learning - working together; this term is often interchanged with collaboration

Transitions - the segment of time between activities

Paraprofessionals - teacher's assistants or aides

B. Age-Appropriate Routines and Procedures
Expectations for Young Children
Young children are still developing collaborative skills. Being aware of their limited ability to work in groups, and their need to learn collaborative skills, teachers should structure lessons that:
- include opportunities to work with others
- provide rewards of some sort for working together effectively
- are brief and to the point
- do not penalize students who are developmentally not ready for collaboration
- offer opportunities for those whose collaborative skills are still developing to gain assistance or perform in an alternate way

Expectations for Older Children
Older children should be able to work productively in teams, though developmental delays still exist at this age. Students should work collaboratively to research concepts, explore ideas, define goals and assessment criteria, and solve problems. Because learning to work with others is a critical life skill, group work is an expectation for all subject areas.

The Strangeness of Adolescence
Cooperative learning has particular challenges when working with adolescents. Teachers should be aware of the importance of peers and peer acceptance when planning lessons. While students should still be working together and collaborating, sensitivity means attention to groups, awareness of group behaviors, and assignments that do not conflict with group acceptance.

C. Teaching Collaboration
Why It Is Important
According to the Partnership for 21st Century Learning, communication and collaboration are important skills that students need to be successful in the work place. Many adults who lose their jobs do so because they failed to learn to work well with others.

How It Looks In a Classroom
Students should be grouped in pairs or small groups (2-5) to:
- identify problems
- brainstorm
- research
- create graphic organizers, thinking maps, and presentations
- work on problems
- discuss concepts
- decide on criteria by which their works are evaluated
- evaluate their works, the works of their peers, and the works of professionals and researchers

Roles and Responsibilities
As students work together, it is important that all members of the group are held accountable for the group's performance. Accountability must be present for all lessons. One method is to provide two grades for each project—one for individual performance and one for the group project as a whole.

continued

6. Management Issues

In addition to accountability, students must learn to function in different roles within a team, roles such as:

- Reporter
- Materials manager
- Checker
- Time-keeper
- Leader
- Editor
- Elaborator
- Secretary

D. A Balanced Schedule

In a classroom, there is a time for everything. Staying too long on a topic or activity can lead to misbehavior. Because of students' shorter attention spans, teachers must plan activities that offer opportunities for:

- Play
- Movement
- Projects
- Learning centers
- Integration

E. Managing Materials and Time

Why It Is Important

One of the biggest challenges today's students face has nothing to do with academic content. In today's frantic society, more than ever before, students struggle with organizational skills. Students may have strong thinking skills and excellent academic knowledge, but may make poor grades because they cannot get to class with the proper materials, keep track of their assignments, and get work turned in on time. Lack of organizational skills can affect every aspect of a child's academic career.

As educators, teaching our pupils to organize their work and materials effectively can strongly affect their academic success. Below are some specific strategies to help students become proficient managers of their materials, work and time.

Materials and Time Management Strategies

- Provide structure and routine.
- Encourage students to solve problems with minimal teacher involvement.
- Assign the student who struggles a classroom buddy.
- Encourage the use of checklists.
- Teach the students memory aides.
- Model the way to approach a project or assignment.
- Require students to use a three-ring binder.
- Have students use a container for small items.
- Have students keep their work in folders.
- Teach students how to keep a neat desk.
- Build desk-cleaning time into the class schedule.
- Encourage students to be responsible for their materials.
- Have a class discussion in which students share their ideas about keeping organized.
- Praise and reward students for improved organization.
- Have classroom jobs and assigned roles.
- Use routines and procedures—particularly for lining up, emergency situations, distributing or collecting materials.

F. Managing Transitions

Why It Is Important

Transitions are those times when the class is shifting from one activity to another. In these moments, disorder and chaos—and therefore misbehavior and injury—are most likely to occur. Managing transitions allows teachers to maximize learning time, and minimize disruptions. Organization and pre-planning is the key.

Transition Strategies

- Provide students with clear ending and beginning times.
- Provide students with a warning that transition is soon to occur (i.e., "You have five more minutes and then it's time for math.").
- Have clear routines and procedures.

6. Management Issues

● ●

Domain II:
Competencies 5-6

- Pay attention to students who have special needs or who do not handle transition well. Take measures to help and prevent issues for these students.
- Post and adhere to schedules.
- Have clear rules and expectations, and review these frequently.
- Follow an active endeavor with a quiet activity (such as, read for five minutes after you return from lunch).

G. Balancing Instructional and Non-Instructional Activities

Why It Is Important

Many non-instructional activities are part of the job and daily life of a teacher—taking attendance, helping students with needs, preparing supplies, handling paperwork. None can deny that these tasks are important. However, instruction is our primary purpose. How can teachers balance all of these tasks?

Creating a Balance

- Utilize planning periods effectively.
- Arrive early to set up materials.
- Plan time for tasks when the students are engaged in self-guided work. However, do not allow yourself to become too absorbed to monitor or help the children.
- Gain assistance from paraprofessionals, volunteers, and responsible students (after their work is complete, not instead of learning).
- Be aware that instruction is our primary purpose —never let administrative tasks supersede teaching children.
- Try to complete paperwork as soon as you can. Once it is off your desk, it has less chance of becoming lost or forgotten.
- Use technology to speed administrative tasks - grade book, attendance, communication.

H. Working with Paraprofessionals and Volunteers

Teacher's aides and volunteers should be a welcome addition to your classroom. They can:
- Provide individual help and attention to needy students.
- Help with administrative tasks.
- Create displays.
- Grade student work.
- Provide scaffolding for low-performing students and students with special needs.

The keys to effective work with volunteers and paraprofessionals are
- Communication
- Respect
- Manners
- Appreciation
- Clear expectations
- Monitoring

Remember, even if others help, you are responsible for what happens in your classroom, and you will be held accountable—so check your helpers to be sure their work enhances your learning community.

I. Promoting Appropriate and Ethical Behavior

One of the most important aspects of classroom management is setting the tone and teaching students how to behave in an appropriate and ethical manner. Steps for success include:
- Communicating high expectations for behavior
- Modeling appropriate interactions
- Having the students help develop classroom rules and procedures
- Holding students accountable for their choices
- Providing clear consequences for breaking the rules
- Consistently enforcing these consequences in a fair manner
- Encouraging students to monitor their own behavior and to become self-managers of their behavior
- Teaching conflict management skills
- Rewarding improvements and successes
- Responding appropriately to misbehaviors

continued

Notes

· ·

6. Management Issues

J. Behavior Management Techniques

Most behavior issues can be prevented. These *proactive methods* can ward off most behavior challenges:

- Arrange seating and group students based on emotional and social needs as well as academic needs.
- Adjust schedules to balance between highly structured activities and lively activities.
- Preplan and organize for success. Pay close attention to transitions. Keep your room and supplies organized.
- Establish a group plan for behavior, including consequences.
- Consistently enforce expectations.
- Monitor student interactions. Move among groups and create an expectation of oversight.
- Avoid overstimulation of students. Keep disruptive activities to the end of the day.
- Show empathy and respect for all students.

Create a relationship of mutual respect.

- Much misbehavior is geared toward gaining attention or power. Give students attention before they act out. One minute of personal conversation can prevent many minutes of misbehavior. Give students choices. Having some measure of control over their learning provides a sense of personal power—and when successful, a sense of personal accomplishment.
- Promote and reward positive behaviors.
- Always be consistent and fair.
- Avoid correcting or praising students publicly. Instead, correct or praise behaviors privately.
- Keep students busy!

Tips from Veteran Teachers:

- Pre-sharpen pencils.
- Minimize out of seat time by having students keep trash at their table until clean-up time.
- Start the day with a pencil/paper activity to calm students down and get them focused.
- Use assigned seating and switch seats as often as necessary.

- Post expectations.
- Communicate with parents about both positive and negative behaviors.
- Keep work handy for those who finish assignments quickly.

K. Classroom Management and Special Education

Students in special education have different discipline needs. Many websites can provide support for helping these students, but your best resources are the parents and the special education teacher.

Much misbehavior occurs because the student's needs are not being met. A few effective strategies:

- Allow extra time for assignments.
- Provide information in a variety of ways.
- Give work in segments (chunking) to prevent overwhelming the student.
- Allow the student to move when necessary.
- Group the student with supportive, patient students.
- Allow "wait time"—a few moments to think before answering questions.
- Provide a place for the student to calm down.

Domain III:

Implementing Effective, Responsive Instruction and Assessment

Competencies 7-10

(31% of the test)

Pedagogy and Professional Responsibilities Standard I:
The teacher designs instruction appropriate for all students that reflects an understanding of relevant content and is based on continuous and appropriate assessment.

Pedagogy and Professional Responsibilities Standard III:
The teacher promotes student learning by providing responsive instruction that makes use of effective communication techniques, instructional strategies that actively engage students in the learning process, and timely, high-quality feedback.

Technology Application Standards I-V:
I.   All teachers use technology-related terms, concepts, data input strategies, and ethical practices to make informed decisions about current technologies and their applications.

II. All teachers identify task requirements, apply search strategies, and use current technology to efficiently acquire, analyze, and evaluate a variety of electronic information.

III. All teachers use task-appropriate tools to synthesize knowledge, create and modify solutions, and evaluate results in a way that supports the work of individuals and groups in problem-solving situations.

IV. All teachers communicate information in different formats and for diverse audiences.

V.   All teachers know how to plan, organize, deliver, and evaluate instruction for all students that incorporates the effective use of current technology for teaching and integrating the Technology Applications Texas Essential Knowledge and Skills (TEKS) into the curriculum.

7. Communication

Group Activity Day

Key Descriptors:

_____

_____

_____

_____

_____

_____

_____

_____

_____

_____

_____

_____

_____

_____

_____

Key Words:

Communication

Questioning

Active Student Inquiry

Higher Order Thinking

Wait Time

Interpersonal Skills

Verbal and Non-verbal Communication

NOTE: Refer to the bullet points under each Competency in the NES/SBEC study guide. Analyze each bullet point, and synthesize it down to a paraphrase that is meaningful to you, using no more than 5-6 words. List those phrases in order on the lines above. It may help to number the bullet points and the lines above. When complete, record them again on Worksheet 4 in Appendix I.

D E S C R I P T O R   H I G H L I G H T S

- Teaches concepts in a clear way that is appropriate to the students' ages, interests, and backgrounds.
- Uses skilled questioning and discussion techniques.
- Fosters active student inquiry, higher order thinking skills, problem solving, and supportive interactions.

- Communicates directions, explanations, and procedures effectively.
- Adjusts communication to enhance student understanding.
- Uses effective communication techniques and interpersonal skills.
- Uses verbal and non-verbal communication, and technology.

7. Communication

Competency 7:

The teacher understands and applies principals and strategies for communicating effectively in varied teaching and learning contexts.

A. Some Important Terms To Know

Student Inquiry - Inquiry is simply questions. Student inquiries occur when students form questions about academic concepts and are driven to find answers to their questions. Inquiry drives the learning.

Higher Order Thinking Skills - Higher order thinking skills are being able to think and process information beyond basic concept memory and recall, to be able to evaluate and utilize information learned.

Bloom's Taxonomy - Bloom's Taxonomy is a classification of higher order thinking skills summarized by Benjamin Bloom in 1956. Bloom's educational research has changed the face of classroom learning and is considered to be a foundational understanding for teachers. In short, we need students who are able to do more than remember what they have learned—this type of learning is not useful. Students must be able to use what they know, to expand upon it, and to branch out into new ideas.

Bloom's Taxonomy

Original Version as Defined by Bloom	Revised Version
Knowledge Comprehension Application Analysis Synthesis Evaluation	Remember Understand Apply Analyze Evaluate Create

Teachers can help their students reach the highest levels of Bloom's Taxonomy by allowing them to cooperatively discuss content and participate in project-based learning. -->The state considers this educational research to be very important. Many questions on the test focus on teachers using higher order thinking skills.<--

B. Communicating Clearly to the Students in Your Classroom

Please note again that we are teaching students, not content. Your instructional communication should be clear to the students. Focus on individual learners, each child's unique skills, interests, and background.

C. Skilled Questioning

Questioning is an essential monitoring strategy. It provides feedback to teachers on the adequacy of their instruction, the learning that has occurred, and areas that require remediation.
1. The Importance of a Classroom Climate that Encourages Questioning
Without a classroom climate that encourages

inquiry and risk-taking, little critical, creative, or higher level thinking can take place. Effective educators build a climate of openness where students feel free to express and try out ideas. Such a climate promotes mutual respect and acceptance and is free of ridicule and sarcasm. Students' efforts are recognized and encouraged. In an environment that stimulates essential questioning, no one has the right answer all the time. Students and teachers become problem solvers together. To create a nurturing climate of this nature, teachers must:
-   establish a rapport with students
-   value, praise and encourage inquiry
-   keep interactive lines of communication open

continued

7. Communication

• •

- model questioning behavior, including the willingness to admit to not having all the answers
- accept student ideas and input; all contributions are accepted without judgment
- establish generating a large number of ideas and questions as a goal
- encourage building on other people's ideas
- welcome outrageous, far-out, and unusual ideas
- foster academic risk-taking
- share personal insights and experiences
- capitalize on student interests, talents and abilities to enrich the curriculum
- model and teach self-reflection skills.

2. Questioning Provides Feedback to the Teacher and the Student

High-quality monitoring through the use of essential questions provides valuable feedback to both the teacher and the learner. Teachers utilize this feedback to evaluate:

- the effectiveness of their teaching
- the level of understanding the students have gained
- what remedial measures are necessary to assure that all students obtain mastery of the lesson's objectives

Effective evaluation of feedback, coupled with timely, sensitive remediation, increase student success. In addition to helping teachers plan for learning and remediation, questioning provides teachers with encouraging feedback when they see the progression of their students.

Students use questioning as an opportunity to:

- demonstrate their skills
- obtain missing information gaps

Demonstrations of successful learning create positive student attitudes, giving them a sense of accomplishment and progression.

3. Questioning Procedures to Stimulate Curiosity and Independent Reasoning

Highly effective teachers encourage students to think critically by asking essential questions. Instead of memorizing facts or looking up answers, students must conduct research and create original answers. Essential questions:

- provoke deep thought
- solicit information-gathering and evaluation of data
- result in an original answer
- help students conduct problem-related research
- make students produce original ideas rather than predetermined answers
- do not have a right or wrong answer
- expect students to defend their answers
- focus on thoughts, conclusions, inferences, and beliefs

When students are challenged with essential questions, they stay on task because they are so intent on answering the question that they have no time to do anything else!

Essential questioning is based on replacing "what" questions with "how", "why", and "what if" questions. "How" and "why" questions require more than a simple yes or no answer. "Why?"—the favorite question of four year-olds—requires analysis of cause-and-effect and the relationship between variables. "Why" questions lead to problem-solving or to decision-making. "How" questions are the basis for problem-solving and synthesis, using questions to stimulate change. "How" is the inventor's favorite question, and inspires us to search for upgrades and enhancements. It is the driving force behind new tools and successful ventures of many types.

4. Questioning Methods and Example Strategies

- Ask well-crafted, open-ended questions.
- Assure that your questions cover only content that has been taught.

7. Communication

- Phrase questions in non-confusing language.
- Ask challenging, uncluttered questions.
- Learn to wait. Give students a moment to think, and give ideas a moment to form.
- Think about the questions that students are asking and make note of what parts of the lesson don't seem to be understood.
- Ask questions from various levels of Bloom's taxonomy of learning objectives.
- Walk around the class and check worksheets, calling attention to errors and noting good work being done.
- Have students do quick problems on individual whiteboards.
- Encourage children to listen to each other by summarizing comments of others.
- Call on children who don't seem to be listening.
- Use short questions and quizzes that require students to demonstrate or explain lesson concepts to verify their understanding of material covered.
- Carefully formulate questions to provide an appropriate level of difficulty, to provide the majority of students a high degree of success.
- Make note of who is answering questions and call upon students who fail to volunteer, giving all children a chance to respond.
- When a student seems to need a moment to think, tell them you will come back to them in a few minutes, taking the pressure off so they can formulate a good answer.
- Ask students to comment on or elaborate on their peers' answers.
- Have students write their own test.
- Ask students to write three comparison questions about the story they are reading.
- Have students find the most interesting question left unanswered by the reading.
- Ask students to identify the question the author was trying to answer.
- Have your class write a question that will demand at least ten minutes of thought to answer.

- Challenge students to find a question which has no answer, or two thousand answers or an infinite number of answers.
- Ask students to identify the most important and the least important questions in a preview, review or test.
- Ask students to interpret or summarize material presented to them in the lesson.
- Ask students to act things out or to draw them.

There have always been plenty of questions in school but most of them have come from the teacher. Often questions are aimed at recall rather than requiring higher level thought. Effective questions are the foundation of discovery, competence, engaged learning, and information literacy.

The most important questions of all are those asked by students as they try to make sense out of content and information. These are the questions which enable students to become powerful decision makers—the leaders of tomorrow

D. Communication Tools

Using technology to communicate lessons is very important. In addition to being highly engaging, technology supports a variety of learning styles and needs. There is more information about technology as a communication tool in Competency 9.

E. Verbal and Non-Verbal Communication

Be aware of your body language as you teach. Students notice when your tone shifts, when you look impatient, or when you are not really interested in what they have to say. Body language can be a tool—a little theatrics can go a long way toward engaging students. Body language can also undermine the relationship and rapport you have worked to create with your students.

8. Engaging Instruction

Key Descriptors:

_____

_____

_____

_____

_____

_____

_____

_____

_____

_____

_____

_____

_____

_____

_____

_____

NOTE: Refer to the bullet points under each Competency in the NES / SBEC study guide. Analyze each bullet point, and synthesize it down to a paraphrase that is meaningful to you, using no more than 5-6 words. List those phrases in order on the lines above. It may help to number the bullet points and the lines above. When complete, record them again on Worksheet 4 in Appendix I.

Key Words:

Varied Teacher-student Roles

Active Engagement

Flexible Grouping

Pacing

Monitoring

Motivation

Self-Motivation

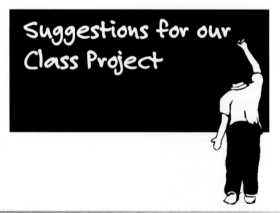

Suggestions for our Class Project

DESCRIPTOR HIGHLIGHTS

- Employs instructional strategies and varies student-teacher roles to promote engagement.
- Promotes engagement by structuring lessons effectively, using flexible grouping, adjusting pacing to student needs, allowing wait-time.
- Presents concepts that are relevant and meaningful.

- Evaluate materials and activities to assure they meet the students' needs.
- Monitors the effectiveness of instruction.
- Motivates students.
- Encourages students to be self-motivated.

8. Engaging Instruction

Competency 8:

The teacher provides appropriate instruction that actively engages students in the learning process.

A. Instructional Techniques

One state expectation for today's Texas classrooms is *student-centered learning mimics modern work teams*. Teachers do not always stand at the front of the room and lecture. Students no longer exclusively sit quietly at desks and take notes or read the textbook. Active, engaged students set their own learning goals and participate all along the pathway to learning. Active classrooms are noisy (but not chaotic), filled with purposeful conversation about academic concepts. Instructional techniques in today's classroom include:

- Discussion - Students should be given the opportunity to discuss ideas, events, concepts, beliefs, etc.
- Inquiry - Students should make predictions, build hypotheses, make inferences, develop essential questions, and seek answers to their questions.
- Problem-solving - Students should identify problems and resources for solutions, and research and solve these problems.
- Varied teacher-student roles - Students learn best what they are allowed to teach; for this to happen, students must take on the role of presenter, researcher, instruction designer, and teachers must step back and become facilitators.
- Intellectual Involvement - Students' bright minds should be inspired in every stage of the learning process. Never dumb-down lessons; instead allow the student new ways to find success and understanding.
- Active Engagement - Active engagement occurs when students direct their own learning. Teachers must be willing to let the students have a measure of control over their

learning, a say in what they are learning and how it will be learned. Students must be allowed to work together on active, hands-on projects.

B. Promoting Learning

- Structuring Lessons Effectively
  Effective lessons move from concept to concept in an orderly fashion. Each idea builds upon previous learning and connects to essential (important) questions.

- Using Flexible Grouping
  Students gain from grouping that is adapted to their specific needs. Flexible grouping is a strategy that allows student groups to change depending upon the problem or activity. Students are grouped sometimes by skill, sometimes by interest, and sometimes purely randomly. Students move to different groups depending on the subject matter being covered. This method gives students wide exposure to diversity and a chance to work with others who share their learning styles or interests.

- Using Flexible Pacing
  Instructional pacing is the speed at which concepts and activities are presented. To maintain student engagement, teachers must maximize the pace of instruction—keep the lessons moving, while still being certain that no one has fallen by the wayside.

- Allowing Wait Time
  Another way to say wait time is "think time". Basically, when students have a concept or question before them, they may need a few moments (2-3 seconds) to think before answering. When teachers allow students *continued*

8. Engaging Instruction

time to think before responding, students tend to:
- Answer with more confidence and more correctly
- Feel more confident in their answers
- Be less inclined to say "I don't know"
- Provide more complex input
- Ask additional, meaningful questions

C. Relevant and Meaningful Lessons

Relevant and meaningful lessons engage students. If what one is learning doesn't matter, there is little motivation to learn it well. The best lessons:
- Link with prior knowledge
- Make connections to life
- Are meaning
- Use real-world examples

D. Evaluating Appropriateness

Materials should be appropriate for all learners. When selecting activities and materials, teachers should consider the specific needs of their students and use this knowledge to select activities that will inspire the learners in their classroom.

E. Evaluating Effectiveness

An important element of success in teaching is evaluating success. If your students cannot demonstrate what they have learned, the lessons were not effective—and must be modified, then repeated. Students demonstrate that lessons were effective by:
- answering questions correctly
- performing correctly on class work and home work
- being able to create projects based on their learning
- being able to hold advanced discussion on the concepts they have learned
- successfully passing examinations

The careful monitoring of student learning is an essential component of high-quality education, a factor that differentiates effective schools and teachers from ineffective ones. Questioning is an essential monitoring strategy. It provides feedback to teachers on the adequacy of their instruction, the learning that has occurred, and areas that require remediation.

F. Types of Motivation

- Intrinsic motivation comes from within. It is an internal drive to do well and to succeed. Intrinsically motivated students draw pleasure from their educational pursuits and find happiness in getting right answers, solving problems, and doing their best.

- Extrinsic motivation comes from outside of one's self. In other words, it is a motivator that comes to you from another person. The most common extrinsic motivators in schools are grades, praise, and reward systems.

One of the most highly effective tools for creating motivated learners is praise. Praising the student (privately) based on a specific action or accomplishment validates learners. Positive notes and reward letters that students can take home help boost self-esteem, and students really respond to teacher comments and immediate feedback in their journals and on their writing and homework. Finally, a system of tangible, positive rewards is also very helpful.

While you certainly don't want to create a dependency on "carrots," tangible rewards are useful tools for teachers and provide a physical reminder of a job well done for hard-working students.
Examples include:
- Prize bin
- Ticket jars
- Homework passes
- Awards

G. Self-Motivation

The goal of teaching is to combine together students who are self-motivated learners, self-driven to set behavioral and educational goals, who produce their best quality work, who are able to evaluate their own performance, and who constantly seek improvement. If you create a classroom environment that is rich with student input, has student work displayed and has the "feel" of a home away from home, your students will enjoy their time in their space. They will take ownership of the place

8. Engaging Instruction

you have created together and will take pride in the work they do while there. Through cooperative learning teams, you can create reliance on each other and accountability that fosters the strength of unity. Students will see and correct their own behavior and work errors, and will utilize positive peer pressure to inspire increased productivity and best effort performance.

9. Technology

Key Descriptors:

_____

_____

_____

_____

_____

_____

_____

_____

_____

_____

_____

_____

_____

_____

_____

_____

Key Words:
Basic Terms and Concepts
    of Current Technology

Acceptable Use

Legal and Ethical
    Guidelines

Word Processing, Spread-
    sheets, Databases

Graphic Tools, Electronic
    Communication

Multimedia Presentations

NOTE: Refer to the bullet points under each Competency in the NES/SBEC study guide. Analyze each bullet point, and synthesize it down to a paraphrase that is meaningful to you, using no more than 5-6 words. List those phrases in order on the lines above. It may help to number the bullet points and the lines above. When complete, record them again on Worksheet 4 in Appendix I.

D E S C R I P T O R   H I G H L I G H T S

- Demonstrates knowledge of technology terms and concepts.
- Knows difference between database and spreadsheet.
- Understands issues related to legal and ethical use of technology.
- Can evaluate technology projects.

- Uses task-appropriate tools to plan, create, communicate, and contribute.
- Uses productivity tools such as slide shows, multimedia, video, etc.
- Addresses equity issues related to use of technology.

9. Technology

Competency 9:

The teacher incorporates the effective use of technology to plan, organize, deliver and evaluate instruction for all students.

A. Basic Technology Terms
- Hardware - the physical components of computers (hard drive, keyboard, mouse, mother board, processors, RAM, monitor, etc.)
- Software - any program or application run within the computer system (Windows operating system, video game, Microsoft Office, etc.)
- Input/Output Devices - a type of hardware used to receive or supply some form of information to the computer operating system; a connection between the user and the computer (keyboard, mouse, speakers, monitor)
- Networks - a connection between multiple computers. This can be a direct connection from one computer to a second, a connection of dozens of computers within a company, or the linking of millions of computers to form the Internet.

B. Types of Technology
All of the following are technology available to teachers:
- Computers
- Audio (CDs, MP3s, etc.)
- Visual (DVD, streaming video, etc.)
- Overhead images
- Internet resources
- Presentations
- Human resources (user groups, field trips, presenters, etc.)

C. Why Technology?
In an increasingly technological world, students who do not learn to use technology effectively are held back. Teachers also need skills with technology to communicate effectively and in a timely manner. Finally, technology is highly engaging to students. Students should be exposed to:

- Word processing
- Spreadsheets
- Desktop publishing
- Internet resources for research and communication
- Paint and graphic programs
- Multimedia presentations

D. How Teachers Can Use Technology
Knowing how to use technology to plan, organize, deliver and evaluate instruction in your classroom will bring your lessons to life. With your skill and assistance, your students will attain a deeper understanding of all subjects, and will build projects that sparkle! Teachers should use technology:

- to prepare—gather information (build personal background, research)
- to provide visuals or auditory examples
- lesson planning (templates, lesson plans of others, rubrics)
- to get supplies (ordering, sharing, locating, freebies, grants)
- to communicate (e-mail to communicate with colleagues, parents)
- parent communication (graphic programs for newsletters, flyers, awards)
- to learn (online staff development, online training programs and college courses, quality research sites, collaborative resources)
- to teach
- to organize and document (grade books, online attendance, etc.)

Technology is the ultimate tool for providing information in a variety of formats: slide shows, multimedia presentations, videos, newsletters.

Domain III: Competencies 7-10

9. Technology

● ●

E. How Students Can Use Technology

Computers can be valuable in many ways. An outstanding variety of educational software that is  both appealing and assistive is available at little or no cost. In addition to computer-aided instruction (drill and practice, tutorials, and simulations), students should use computers for:

1. Self-guided instruction and tutorials

2. Research
    - Websites for children
    - Online dictionaries and encyclopedias
    - Homework help
    - Presentation/final drafts/publication

3. Enrichment and reinforcement
    When technology is used effectively, student attention, participation, and retention show marked improvement.

4. Polishing Student Work
    Nothing provides a sense of accomplishment like a beautifully polished product. Computer-generated reports, portfolios, and other projects increase student involvement and self-esteem. No matter where they go in life, the technological processes and skills students learn in the classroom will contribute to future opportunities and life skills.

5. Developing Higher Order Thinking Skills
    Task-appropriate tools and procedures yield higher order thinking skills. Students should use technology to synthesize knowledge, create and modify solutions, evaluate results in problem-solving situations, and for project-based learning.

F. Ethical Use

When using technology, it is very important to avoid violating copyright laws and plagiarism. An understanding of legal and ethical guidelines regarding technology usage is imperative for educators. A commitment to ethical technology use will save you, your school, and your school district from embarssing and expensive problems.

Be aware of:
- Privacy guidelines (students must learn to safe guard personal information)
- Copyright laws (information here: http://home.earthlink.net/~cnew/research.htm)
- Fair Use guidelines
- Acceptable Use policies (set by districts)

G. Evaluating Information

All technology brought into the classroom must be evaluated for appropriateness for the students in your classroom. Materials should be:
- Relevant
- Developmentally appropriate
- Accurate
- Valid
- Useful in building problem-solving skills, decision-making skills, and higher order thinking skills
- Emphasize collaboration and teamwork
- Useful for integrating the Technology TEKS (Familiarity with the Technology TEKS can help you select the correct answers on your exam. These TEKS can be downloaded here: http://ritter.tea.state.tx.us/rules/tac/chapter126/index.html)

H. Evaluating Technologically Produced Projects

Student projects should be assessed for:
- Design
- Content delivery
- Audience
- Relevance for assignment

9. Technology

● ●

I. **Equity**

Many students come from home environments that lack technology. When creating assignments, teachers should be sensitive to providing assignments that can be performed equitably. The best solutions offer students the opportunity to work with others (to support lack of skills) and to work at school or with school-loaned technology. Having a student do an alternate project may occasionally be necessary, but it is not a best choice as this student is denied the opportunity to develop technological skills.

J. **Selecting Correct Answers**

The best choices on this test will involve:

- Students working collaboratively
- Teachers demonstrating concepts using primary resources and authentic discovery learning from Internet resources
- Students selecting, evaluating, and creating technology-based projects
- Students being allowed equitably (fair) access to computers and other technology

10. Assessment

Key Descriptors:

_____

_____

_____

_____

_____

_____

_____

_____

_____

_____

_____

_____

_____

_____

_____

_____

_____

NOTE: Refer to the bullet points under each Competency in the NES/SBEC study guide. Analyze each bullet point, and synthesize it down to a paraphrase that is meaningful to you, using no more than 5-6 words. List those phrases in order on the lines above. It may help to number the bullet points and the lines above. When complete, record them again on Worksheet 4 in Appendix I.

Key Words:
Assessment Methods
Assessment Criteria
Timely, Effective Feedback
Self-Assessment

Bell-shaped Curve

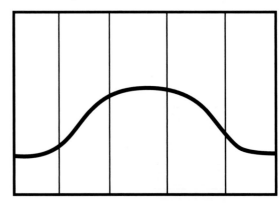

D E S C R I P T O R   H I G H L I G H T S

- Understands the purposes and format of various testing methods.
- Creates tests that match instructional goals.
- Communicates test criteria to students clearly, demonstrating high expectations.

- Provides clear, useful feedback.
- Teaches students to self-assess.
- Adjusts instruction based on test data.

10. Assessment

Competency 10:

The teacher monitors student performance and achievement; provides students with timely, high-quality feedback; and responds flexibly to promote learning for all students.

A. Purposes and Types of Assessment

Assessments can be easily divided into two categories: informal and formal.

1. Informal assessments are generally instructor-designed. As the name suggests, these assessments are less systematic and regimented than conventional assessments. Informal tests include:
   - teacher observations of student body language during questioning
   - the types of questions the students themselves are asking
   - work samples such as daily work
   - portfolios.

Advantages
   - often are visual
   - provide immediate feedback on the effectiveness of daily instructional tasks and activities
   - allow the instructor to quickly adapt presentation to increase student performance
   - easy to adjust without extensive planning and preparation time
   - can provide a more clear image of the abilities of certain student populations (disabled, second-language learners, students who don't perform well under the pressures of formal testing)
   - provide the instructor with solid information about emotional, social, and motivational factors which affect students' learning

The greatest advantages of informal tests are their practicality in regard to preparation and grading time, and their adaptability to student and situational needs.

Disadvantages
   - results can be unreliable if not coupled with formal assessment
   - lack standardization
   - do not reflect accurately for some students (shy, other social factors)
   - portfolios and projects can be influenced by student creativity and social factors (availability of materials, parental assistance)

2. Formal assessments are more regimented and structured. Formal assessments are in general less forgiving than informal assessments. However, they provide specific information about student knowledge that cannot be gained through informal assessment alone. These assessments can be either norm-referenced or criterion-referenced. A norm-referenced examination compares a student's performance to other students' who have taken the test. For example, the ITBS (Iowa Test of Basic Skills), a test of basic skills, measures a student's national percentile rank (NPR) and compares their score with those of others in his/her grade in the nation. This information is important, as it measures students' knowledge and skills, and creates a mean average for student performance. They are important as they allow instructors to measure competency and knowledge levels in their content areas. Formal tests include:
   - conventional examinations
   - paper and pencil tests
   - end of course exams
   - projects and presentations scored with a rubric

Advantages
   - because the tests are standardized, all students approach the assessment on equal footing (at least theoretically)

Notes

10. Assessment

• •

- provide opportunities to gauge the educational effectiveness of teachers and programs
- provide valid preparation for a lifetime of testing

As adults, we must test to be licensed to drive, to work in many fields, and to advance within many corporations. Teaching students to test without fear, utilizing formal testing as an opportunity to demonstrate one's competency and skills, is a life skill with multiple real-world applications.

Disadvantages

- created by testing experts, but the extreme cost of developing and producing these tests may lead to flaws
- tests are largely multiple choice, which limits demonstration of higher level thinking skills
- test questions may be worded poorly and confusing to the reader
- second-language learners have significant disadvantages, as these tests are rigid and terminology is often slanted toward English-proficient students
- these tests create a high degree of pressure on both instructors and students

B. The Key to Effective Assessment

The key to effective assessment is balance. No single method will address the needs and skills of all learners. As with educational methods, assessment methods must be varied to provide excellent instruction to all students. A totally effective teacher adapts testing to student needs on an individual basis. Effective teachers use a variety of testing methods to assess student learning. Effective teachers help students see assessment as an opportunity to "shine" as opposed to a dreaded evil that must be endured.

The best assessment of student learning involves using a variety of assessments. When using many different observations and types of tests, teachers gain the most accurate snapshot of student learning.

C. Tests and Instructional Goals

Testing must match material that has been taught. Assessments should be aligned with teaching objectives.

D. Explaining Test Criteria

Before testing, students and teachers should work together to define the criteria by which they will be assessed. Having students write their own tests is a powerful tool. In the process of deciding what is important to know, students review and refine their knowledge. Imagine taking your TExES exam without any guidance about what will be covered. Failure to provide students with test criteria is just as unfair as this scenario would be.

E. Providing Useful Feedback

Students need timely feedback. It is good to get graded tests back to students quickly. Be sure to go over the test with students, helping them to see what the right answers were and why. In the process of correcting their answers, misconceptions are repaired and knowledge is gained.

F. Teaching Self-Assessment

Students should be measuring and graphing their own success. Self-assessment is a state expectation. Teaching students to reflect on their performance is a life skill that assists with success in college or the work force.

G. Using Test Data

Testing data should lead teachers to adjust their instruction so that student needs are being met. Use test data to:

- Find concepts to re-teach
- Catalog teaching strategies that worked well
- Uncover areas where students are unengaged and disinterested, and adjust instruction to improve engagement
- Identify learning needs and students requiring additional help

Domain IV:
Fulfilling Professional Roles and Responsibilities

Competencies 11-13

(23% of the test)

Pedagogy and Professional Responsibilities Standard IV:
The teacher fulfills professional roles and responsibilities and adheres to legal and ethical requirements of the profession.

11. Family

Key Descriptors:

_____

_____

_____

_____

_____

_____

_____

_____

_____

_____

_____

_____

_____

_____

_____

Key Words:

Communication

Engages Families

Interacts Appropriately

Conferences

Support Resources

NOTE: Refer to the bullet points under each Competency in the NES/SBEC study guide. Analyze each bullet point, and synthesize it down to a paraphrase that is meaningful to you, using no more than 5-6 words. List those phrases in order on the lines above. It may help to number the bullet points and the lines above. When complete, record them again on Worksheet 4 in Appendix I.

D E S C R I P T O R   H I G H L I G H T S

- Communicates using appropriate methods including technology.
- Engages caregivers in the educational process.
- Interacts appropriately with families despite diversity.

- Communicates regularly to families and responds to their concerns.
- Conducts effective parent conferences.
- Uses family support services to help families in need.

---

11. Family

Competency 11:

The teacher understands the importance of family involvement in children's education and knows how to interact and communicate effectively with families.

A. Engaging Caregivers

Students spend approximately 40% of their time in the classroom. While this is a large amount of time, the greatest amount of their time is spent at home among their families, extended families, and friends. A student who has educational support at home has increased success in the classroom. For this reason, it is very important to connect with each child's family and to engage the family in providing support at home for classroom instruction.

Families can help by:
- Monitoring homework
- Helping with home practice (flash cards, etc.)
- Reading with the child
- Listening to the child read
- Taking the child to the library and to museums
- Getting books and videos about topics of study
- Encouraging the child in his/her educational efforts
- Providing insight on the child's strengths, struggles, and needs
- Providing rewards or consequences based on school efforts and performance

Parents are our partners in the child's education! It is a team effort.

B. Communicating Effectively and Regularly

The key to good teamwork is communication. Parents need regular communication (daily, weekly) about instructional topics, homework and practice expectations, and student performance (both good and bad). To enhance communication, teachers should:

- Provide clear expectations and goals
- Forge professional relationships with parents by demonstrating understanding, support, and concern
- Communicate concerns, but don't tattle
- Focus on what is needed or expected, not failures ("Mary needs to spend more time practicing" as opposed to "Mary is not doing her work")
- Be understanding about home issues and find solutions instead of problems
- Listen!
- Demonstrate respect

C. Appropriate Interactions

Appropriate interactions begin with respect. In order to build relationships with parents, teachers must avoid the human tendency to judge. Regardless of appearance or social skills, a parent who has made the time to connect with you has done so because they care about the student. Begin your interactions with thankfulness that the parent is involved and cares enough to be a part of the child's education. For successful interactions, you should:

- Never argue with a parent (even if he/she begins the conversation in a combative way).
- Never defend or justify your actions (even if he/she begins the conversation in a combative way).
- Listen and try to understand the parent's point of view or concern.
- Remain positive and calm, even if you feel defensive.
- Look for solutions that meet the needs of the child.

continued

Notes

11. Family

D. Parent Conferences

Effective parent conferences keep the focus on the team collaboration you have built. Some pointers to make your conferences a success:

- Create a friendly setting.
- Keep the tone positive.
- Have a plan of what you'd like to discuss.
- Begin and end with positives—focus on successes and accomplishments.
- Resist the urge to use conferences to "tattle"; behavior should only be the focus when it affects the child's learning.
- Allow the parents time to talk.
- Encourage questions and ask questions that invite parents to share.
- Listen!
- Address parent concerns.
- Provide samples of student work.

E. Finding Support and Resources for Families

One of the most difficult tasks for teachers is finding an effective balance between compassion and professionalism. As we know from human development studies, students' basic needs must be met before they can focus their efforts on learning. To this end, teachers must somehow help parents find resources, both educational and social, to help the student. Some ways you can help:

- Keep a list of agencies that provide social assistance to families; offer the numbers to parents when needed (in a respectful, private way).
- Be aware of organizations that provide holiday gifts as this is a frequent need.
- Find solutions for students who cannot provide their own school supplies—solutions that protect the dignity of the child.
- Allow in-school opportunities for use of technology, resources, and supplies.
- Create projects with a sensitivity to the home environments of all students.
- Keep a lending library of books and supplies.

12. Practitioner

Key Descriptors:

_____

_____

_____

_____

_____

_____

_____

_____

_____

_____

_____

_____

_____

_____

_____

_____

_____

Key Words:

Team Teaching

Vertical and Horizontal Teaming

Mentoring

Supportive Collaboration

Specialists

Chain of Command

Teacher Appraisal

Professional Development

Reflection

INSERVICE TODAY

NOTE: Refer to the bullet points under each Competency in the NES/SBEC study guide. Analyze each bullet point, and synthesize it down to a paraphrase that is meaningful to you, using no more than 5-6 words. List those phrases in order on the lines above. It may help to number the bullet points and the lines above. When complete, record them again on Worksheet 4 in Appendix I.

DESCRIPTOR HIGHLIGHTS

- Interacts appropriately with other professionals.
- Maintains supportive, collaborative relationships with colleagues.
- Knows roles of campus specialists.
- Participates in school activities.
- Uses resources for professional growth.
- Understands teacher appraisal system and uses appraisal to improve skills.

- Builds professional skills by working productively with colleagues.
- Uses professional development resources to enhance knowledge and skills.
- Reflects and self-assesses to build skills, identify challenges, and improve teaching.

12. Practitioner

• •

Competency 12:

The teacher enhances professional knowledge and skills by effectively interacting with other members of the educational community and participating in various types of professional activities.

A. Teaming

Vertical Teaming involves collaborating with colleagues who share your content area across grade levels (i.e., all science teachers from grades 2-5 collaborate, all music teachers from grades 8-12 collaborate, etc.)

Horizontal Teaming involves collaborating with colleagues from different content areas in a single grade level (i.e., all 6th grade teachers—science, ELA, math, social studies—collaborate, etc.)

Team Teaching involves working with teacher partners within the same classroom. Examples of team teaching are:
- Partner teaching (two teachers teach in the same classroom; each has specific curriculum they teach)
- Inclusion teaching (special education teacher assists specific students within a regular class room setting)
- Mentoring (such as student teaching)

Advantages of Teaming:
- Consistent expectations for students
- Opportunities for professional growth and development
- Specialization
- Collaboration
- Ability to utilize data effectively to make results-oriented decisions
- Alignment of written, taught, and tested curriculum
- Creation of a sense of shared responsibility, goals, and beliefs

B. Building Collaborative Relationships

The state expectation for teachers is that we collaborate with colleagues in a supportive, cooperative way—for the benefit of our students. We all have something to learn and something to share. Positive, professional relationships allow us to:
- Support student learning
- Share perspectives, ideas, and solutions
- Work together to achieve campus and district goals
- Enhance your teaching repertoire of skills

C. Specialists

Many administrative and support staff members round out our campus faculty. It is important for new teachers:
- to understand the roles and responsibilities of these professionals
- to understand how these professionals can support classroom teachers and students
- to know when to involve these professionals/seek out their help
- to know how to interact with other professionals in an appropriate, professional way.

Specialists include:
- Department Chair
- Curriculum Coordinator
- Technology Coordinator
- School Counselor
- Special Education Professionals
- Principal
- Board of Trustees

continued

12. Practitioner

D. Participation

When you give of yourself and your personal time, not only do you meet state expectations for teachers and endear yourself to your administrators, you model the care and support you have for your students. They know you are going beyond expectations for them. Your volunteerism and advocacy means is valuable to all concerned. The values of participation are:

- Building a positive influence on the teaching and learning environment
- Being an advocate for your students and their needs
- Creating relationships and demonstrating care for students
- Supporting a learning community
- Becoming an active problem solver
- Collaborating and sharing ideas and solutions

Participation expectations - Texas teachers should participate in:

- Decision-making sessions and activities
- Problem solving strategy meetings
- Collaboration on campus and district issues and goals
- Professional development
- School committees
- School and district events
- Special school projects

E. Professional Development Support Systems and Resources

In addition to meeting state expectations for professional development, teachers should model a lifelong love of learning. Resources for learning opportunities include:

- Mentors
- Service centers
- State initiatives
- Universities
- Support systems
- Conferences
- Online resources
- Professional journals
- Workshops
- Professional associations
- Coursework

F. Teacher Appraisal

Characteristics

The Professional Development and Appraisal System, or PDAS, is the Commissioner's recommended teacher appraisal system. It is the State's approved instrument for appraising teachers and identifying growth opportunities. The PDAS has two components—a teacher self-report and an administrator appraisal based on one or more forty-five minute observations. The PDAS evaluation features 51 observed criteria encompassed within 8 domains:

1. Active, successful student participation in the learning process
2. Learner-centered instruction
3. Evaluation and feedback on student progress
4. Management of student discipline, instructional strategies, time/materials
5. Professional communication
6. Professional development
7. Compliance with policies, operating procedures and requirements
8. Improvement of all students' academic performance

The assessed domains are based on the Proficiencies for Learner-centered Instruction adopted in 1997 by the State Board for Educator Certification (SBEC).

Using Appraisals

Appraisals should be valued, and used to help improve our skills as teachers. On the TExES exam, correct answers regarding appraisals focus on self-reflection and using appraisal data for teaching improvement.

12. Practitioner

G. Working Productively with Supervisors and Colleagues

As teachers, we must model and present the utmost in professional behavior. Professional standards for interactions with supervisors and colleagues include:

- Listening
- Respect
- Keeping the focus on solutions
- Remaining positive
- Addressing issues privately
- Focusing on your sphere of influence
- Demonstrating compliance with management
- Avoiding gossip and drama
- Maintaining confidentiality
- Valuing diversity in your colleagues

H. Reflection

It is in reflection that we become aware of our challenges and successes. For this reason, Texas teachers are expected to engage in regular reflection—in order to become the best we can be for our students.

Focus for reflection:

- Strengths
- Challenges
- Potential problems
- Improve teaching and learning
- Ensure safety
- Prevent behavioral issues

Domain IV: Competencies 11-13

13. Texas Teachers

Key Descriptors:

_____
_____
_____
_____
_____
_____
_____
_____
_____
_____
_____
_____
_____
_____
_____
_____
_____
_____

NOTE: Refer to the bullet points under each Competency in the NES/SBEC study guide. Analyze each bullet point, and synthesize it down to a paraphrase that is meaningful to you, using no more than 5-6 words. List those phrases in order on the lines above. It may help to number the bullet points and the lines above. When complete, record them again on Worksheet 4 in Appendix I.

Key Words:

Special Education

Student and Family Rights

Equity

Student Discipline

Child Abuse

Copyright

Fair Use

Data Security

Privacy

Acceptable Use

Confidentiality

State Education System

Procedures for State Mandated Tests

DESCRIPTOR HIGHLIGHTS

- Knows and adheres to the legal guidelines for Texas educators.
- Follows the law and ethical guidelines relating to technology and resources.
- Knows and follows the Texas Code of Ethics for educators.
- Maintains accurate student records.

- Knows and follows laws and guidelines for administering state assessments.
- Understands the state education system structure, and uses this knowledge to seek information and help.
- Advocates for students and the teaching profession.

13. Texas Teachers

Competency 13:

The teacher understands and adheres to legal and ethical requirements for educators and is knowledgeable of the structure of education in Texas.

A. Special Education Law

Because of IDEA, (Individuals with Disabilities Education Act), special needs students must be placed in the "least restrictive environment." IDEA mandates that whenever possible, disabled children should be educated in regular classrooms. If not possible, then students with special needs must be educated in the setting that provides the maximum opportunity for interaction with non-disabled peers. Many times this means that the student is placed in the regular classroom at least part of the day (known as "mainstreaming", or "inclusion"). Many teachers resist inclusion but it is the law and as a professional, teachers should do their best to make the blended setting successful for all students.

Inclusion is the law—it is not an option. Welcome special needs students and go the extra mile to meet their needs.

Special education students are served by a legal document, the Individual Education Plan, or I.E.P. This document supersedes all curriculum and other requirements—it is a guideline of how this student will be served. More than a guideline, it is a legal, binding document. Teachers are required by law:

- to be knowledgeable of
- to regularly review, and
- to follow the IEP.

> **The I.E.P. is law.**
> **Teachers are legally bound to follow a student's I.E.P.**

B. Gifted Students

Serving gifted students in appropriate ways is another aspect of school law. The Texas Education Code requires that gifted students be:

- Screened – ongoing process, using multiple sources of data, equitable and accessible to all student populations
- Selected – by a committee of at least three educators with advanced Talented and Giftedness (TAG) training
- Provided learning opportunities that meet their needs

Learning options must include:

- instructional and organizational patterns that enable identified students to work together as a group, to work with other students, and to work independently;
- a continuum of learning experiences that leads to the development of advanced-level products and performances;
- in-school and, when possible, out-of-school options relevant to the student's area of strength that are available during the entire school year; and
- opportunities to accelerate in areas of strength.

C. Student and Family Rights

Parents are as important as teachers in the success of education. Parent participation is strongly encouraged in the child's educational program. As educators, teachers are obligated to connect with and involve parents in the education process. To this end, teachers:

- Must make a valiant effort to connect with the families of all students
- Must provide regular communication to families
- Must obtain parental consent for many things, including before a psychological examination, test or treatment is conducted, before a video or recording is made, and before a child's photo or art is published

continued

13. Texas Teachers

- Must keep parents informed of behavioral issues, educational strengths, and needs
- Must not attempt to circumvent parents or limit parental rights
- Must not keep records from parental view

Parents have the right to:
- Have access to all written records (any thing written down is considered a record)
- Review all materials in the classroom
- Review tests after the test is administered
- Have access to any public meeting of the school board
- Request a change in the class or teacher, providing the change does not affect other students
- Request that their child attend a class above the child's grade level
- Request their child graduate from high school earlier if courses required for graduation are completed
- Have full information regarding school activities
- Have copies of easily understood documents regarding special education including their child's ARD (Admission Review Dismissal)
- Appeal the placement of their child in a special education class
- Receive assistance from the school, including counseling, tutorials, and remedial programs
- Obtain information on academic requirements of the school program
- Inspect their child's record and respond to any statement
- Be informed of and to appeal school policies
- Be informed of and to appeal administrative decisions

Parents + Teachers = Success for Children

D. Equity
The demonstration of respect and equity for both students and colleagues impacts all aspects of the learning environment. Unfairness and bias drives students away from school and leaves them feeling harassed. Characteristics that make students enjoy their work and feel safe are:
- Integrity
- Fairness
- Respect

Areas of equity that may be presented on the test:
- Equity to materials
- Equity to technology
- Equity to support services
- Equity to teacher assistance and prompting

E. Child Abuse
Being aware of and reporting child abuse is a very important task for teachers. Teachers represent the front line of defense for children. There are many types of abuse defined by the law:
- Physical
- Sexual
- Emotional/psychological
- Neglect (abandonment, medical neglect, neglectful supervision, physical neglect, refusal to accept parental responsibility-RAPR) — Texas Family Code 261.001

Definitions:
- Child abuse and neglect is defined as any act or omission, inflicted upon a child that causes physical and/or emotional harm.
  — Texas Family Code 261.001

- Domestic violence is physical harm or a threat that places a person in fear of imminent physical harm, bodily injury,

13. Texas Teachers

assault, or sexual abuse. Domestic violence is a criminal offense, not a "private" family matter; it effects families (adults and children) and communities.

• Dating violence is the intentional use of physical, sexual, verbal, or emotional abuse by a person to harm, threaten, intimidate, or control another person in a dating relationship.
— Texas Family Code 71.0021

All Texas teachers are mandated reporters. State law requires that suspected child abuse and neglect be reported to Child Protective Services, local law enforcement, or 911 within 48 hours.
— Texas Family Code 261.101(b)

What to do if you suspect child abuse:
1. Call your district child abuse office immediately
2. Contact
   - CPS Statewide Intake at 1-800-252-5400,
   - Local police department, or
   - 911.

F. Copyright, Fair Use, Data Security, Privacy, and Acceptable Use

Texas teachers must know and adhere to legal and ethical requirements regarding the use of educational resources and technologies (e.g., copyright, fair use, data security, privacy, acceptable use policies).

Failure to follow these guidelines is breaking the law (and prosecutable).

TEA hosts a list of resources on fair use and copyright here:
http://ritter.tea.state.tx.us/technology/techapp/instruct/general/cpyright.htm

G. Code of Ethics

Texas teachers must apply knowledge of ethical guidelines for educators in Texas (e.g., those related to confidentiality, interactions with students and others in the school community), including policies and procedures described in the Code of Ethics and Standard Practices for Texas Educators.

The Code of Ethics and Standard Practices for Texas Educators can be found here:
http://www.tcta.org/capital/sbec/codeapproved.htm

Summary of code regarding students:
• Do not reveal confidential information concerning students unless disclosure serves lawful professional purposes or is required by law.
• Do not treat a student in a manner that adversely affects the student's learning, physical health, mental health or safety.
• Do not deliberately or knowingly misrepresent facts regarding a student.
• Do not exclude a student from participation in a program, deny benefits to a student, or grant an advantage to a student on the basis of race, color, sex, disability, national origin, religion, or family status.
• Do not engage in physical mistreatment of a student.
• Do not solicit or engage in sexual conduct or a romantic relationship with a student.
• Do not furnish alcohol or illegal/unauthorized drugs to any student or knowingly allow any student to consume alcohol or illegal/unauthorized drugs in the presence of the educator

Summary of remainder of the code:
• Do not engage in deceptive practices.
• Do not use school money, personnel, or property for personal gain.

continued

Notes

13. Texas Teachers

- Do not submit fraudulent requests for reimbursement, expenses or pay.
- Do not use institutional or professional privileges for personal or partisan advantage.
- Do not accept nor offer gratuities, gifts, or favors that impair professional judgment or to obtain special advantage (small gifts from students and parents are excluded).
- Do not falsify records, or direct or coerce others to do so.
- Comply with state regulations, written local school board policies and other applicable state and federal laws.
- Hire only on the basis of professional qualifications.
- Do not reveal confidential health or personnel information concerning colleagues.
- Do not harm others by knowingly making false statements about a colleague or the school system.
- Adhere to written local school board policies and state and federal laws regarding the hiring, evaluation, and dismissal of personnel.
- Do not interfere with a colleague's exercise of political, professional or citizenship rights and responsibilities.
- Do not discriminate against or coerce a colleague on the basis of race, color, religion, national origin, age, sex, disability, or family status.
- Do not use coercive means or promise of special treatment in order to influence professional decisions or colleagues.
- Do not retaliate against any individual who has filed a complaint with the SBEC under this chapter.

H. Maintaining Accurate Student Records
Texas teachers must follow procedures and requirements for maintaining accurate student records.

This includes attendance, grading, SPED, TAG, etc.—as well as lesson planning.

I. Administering State Assessments
Texas teachers must understand the importance of and adhere to required procedures for administering state- and district-mandated assessments.

Testing regulations are very serious. The ramifications for failure to follow guidelines—to the student, the school, and the teacher—are severe.

J. The State Education System
Texas teachers must understand the relationship among campus, local, and state components. Teachers should use their knowledge of the structure of the state education system, including relationships among campus, local, and state components, to seek information and assistance. In other words, teachers should be aware of, and follow the chain of command.

K. Advocating for Students and for the Profession
Texas teachers must advocate for students and for the profession in various situations.
- Serve as an advocate for all children.
- Promote continuous and appropriate development of all students.
- Support the development of teacher candidates and the teaching profession.

Go the extra mile to find the help your students need. Listen to students and parents. Work together to find solutions. Offer tutorials. Seek help from other professionals and refer students to agencies that can help.

Appendix I

Tips and Study Aids

NOTE: The pages in Appendix I may be duplicated.

Tips for Test Day

1. There are two five-hour testing periods in a day; you need to request one test per testing period or schedule your PPR and your content area test on separate days if possible.

2. Get to the exam an hour or two early; the directions they send out are usually a little confusing, and you don't want to be rushed or upset.

3. Take two forms of ID, one has to have your picture on it.

4. Take three or more number 2 pencils.

5. Bring a receipt or any other form of confirmation of registration you might have.

6. During the practice tests and the real tests mark the important details in both the questions and the answers. Always mark any questions you are not sure of.

7. As soon as the exam is handed to you, divide the total amount of questions by 5 hours. If you have 100 questions, then you only have to answer 20 questions per hour.

8. Write down your acronym (see p. 92) and brief Competency information on your test booklet prior to the test. When answering each question, refer to the acronym and write down the Competency number by each exam question.

9. Read all of the answers before making your selection.

10. Always know the Competency the question is referring to before answering the question.

11. Answers to questions: Two are remotely correct and two are reasonably correct. Use your critical thinking skills and pick the best answer.

13. After you complete the test there is usually plenty of time to double-check your answers. Always put a mark of some type beside any answers you are not sure of, so that afterward you can double-check your responses.

IMPORTANT NOTE: Follow the "Steps for Success" on pages 10 and 11 of this manual.

Appendix I
Tips and Study Aids

Acronym

This study program involves the use of an acronym for easy memorization. If the acronym below is not to your liking, simply change it to an acronym that works for you.

NOTE:

> **DOMAIN I has 4 Competencies: 1-4** *(31% of the test)*
> **DOMAIN II has 2 Competencies: 5-6** *(15% of the test)*
> **DOMAIN III has 4 Competencies: 7-10** *(31% of the test)*
> **DOMAIN IV has 3 Competencies: 11-13** *(23% of the test)*

As you use the worksheets keep the acronym in mind—it will help you remember the **Key Titles** for each Competency (example: TEKS, TEchnology, Assessment, etc.). The vertical list of letters below represent the first letter of the first word of each **Key Title**. The titles are descriptive of the Competency, and once you recall the **Title**, the Competency information should come back to you.

DOMAIN I: DESIGNING INSTRUCTION AND ASSESSMENT TO PROMOTE STUDENT LEARNING	1. H	Human
	2. D	Development
	3. T	Teaches
	4. H	How
DOMAIN II: CREATING A POSITIVE, PRODUCTIVE CLASSROOM ENVIRONMENT	5. E	Effective
	6. M	Management
DOMAIN III: IMPLEMENTING EFFECTIVE, RESPONSIVE INSTRUCTION AND ASSESSMENT	7. C	Can
	8. E	Engage.
	9. T	Technology
	10. A	Assesses
DOMAIN IV: FULFILLING PROFESSIONAL ROLES AND RESPONSIBILITIES	11. F	Family
	12. P	Practitioners (in)
	13. T	Texas.

SO...

Human development teaches how effective management can engage.
Technology assesses family practitioners in Texas

NOTE: These acronym-based phrases represent all 13 Competencies.

Copy this chart and carry it with you for easy study.

Competencies

Domain I

1. **Human Development**

Competency 1:
The teacher understands human development processes and applies this knowledge to plan instruction and ongoing assessment that motivate students and are responsible to their developmental characteristics and needs.

2. **Diversity**

Competency 2:
The teacher understand student diversity and knows how to plan learning experiences and design assessments that are responsive to differences among students and that promote all students' learning

3. **TEKS**

Competency 3:
The teacher understands procedures for designing effective and coherent instruction and assessment based on appropriate learning goals and objectives.

4. **How Learning Occurs**

Competency 4:
The teacher understands learning processes and factors that impact student learning and demonstrates this knowledge by planning effective, engaging instruction and appropriate assessments.

Domain II

5. **Environment of Support**

Competency 5:
The teacher knows how to establish a classroom climate that fosters learning, equity, and excellence and uses this knowledge to create a physical and emotional environment that is safe and productive.

6. **Management Issues**

Competency 6:
The teacher understands strategies for creating an organized and productive learning environment and for managing student behavior.

Domain III

7. **Communication**

Competency 7:
The teacher understands and applies principals and strategies for communicating effectively in varied teaching and learning contexts.

8. **Engaging Instruction**

Competency 8:
The teacher provides appropriate instruction that actively engages students in the learning process.

9. **Technology**

Competency 9:
The teacher incorporates the effective use of technology to plan, organize, deliver, and evaluate instruction for all students.

10. **Assessment**

Competency 10:
The teacher monitors student performance and achievement; provides students with timely, high-quality feedback; and responds flexibly to promote learning for all students.

Domain IV

11. **Family**

Competency 11:
The teacher understands the importance of family involvement in children's education and knows how to interact and communicate effectively with families.

12. **Practitioner**

Competency 12:
The teacher enhances professional knowledge and skills by effectively interacting with other members of the educational community and participating in various types of professional activities.

13. **Texas Teachers**

Competency 13:
The teacher understands and adheres to legal and ethical requirements for educators and is knowledgeable of the structure of education in Texas.

Appendix I Tips and Study Aids

Practice Test Method

After using this manual over a period of several weeks you should be able to recall quite a bit of information you have studied about each Competency. Worksheet 5 has a great suggestion for finding out "what you know and what you don't know".

When you can do the preceding you are 50% prepared for the exam.

The last half of your preparation consists of learning how to assess your new found knowledge base. Of course there are practice questions available for the TExES exam in the NES/SBEC study manual, and additional questions may be available from your university, alternative certification program, or school district.

The practice test questions in Appendix III of this manual are a sampling of the NES/SBEC questions but we have added a series of questions in italics to ask yourself after each question. We have also provided a Practice Test Worksheet to accompany the Practice Test...it can be used with any practice test questions you have access to. For a quick review of our Practice Test Worksheet process, see below:

1. **Read each question, and if you wish, restate the question in your own words.** In other words...figure out what they are really asking you. Always read the question and all the choices of answers before restating the question in your own words.

2. **Determine what Competency the question is referring to.** If you look at the answer key to the sample questions in the NES/SBEC manual, you will notice that the Competency number appears beside each answer. Each question refers to a particular Competency in the sample test and on the real test. Knowledge of the Competency information will help you answer questions. However, you must also consider the point of view of the SBEC to help you determine the answers.

3. **State why you think this is the correct Competency.** It is best to understand why you are making your choices. Expressing this in writing is part of your analysis process.

4. **State your answer. State why this is correct answer and why it connects to the Competency you chose.** It is important to understand why you are making the choices you are making.

5. **Look up the Competency and the answer in the answer key after completing each question.** If you missed the answer cross yours out and write the letter of the correct answer beside yours. If you missed the Competency number cross yours out and write the correct one beside that.

6. **Write down why you were wrong about the Competency, or answer, or both, and why the answer key is correct.** This is an important analysis which leads you to an understanding of the point of view of the SBEC. You may not agree with their point of view but choosing the answers that the SBEC would choose is important to your success on the test.

Continue through every question this way and by the end of the practice test you should be getting better at identifying the Competencies and choosing the correct answers.

Worksheet 1
Competency Key Titles

List the first letter of each Key Title for each Competency: (Study them on the Competency study pages, on the Competency Chart, and on the PowerPoint® study module, and then write them from memory here.)

I.   Designing Instruction and Assessment to Promote Student Learning

    1.   _____

    2.   _____

    3.   _____

    4.   _____

II.   Creating a Positive, Productive Classroom Environment

    5.   _____

    6.   _____

III. Implementing Effective, Responsive Instruction and Assessment

    7.   _____

    8.   _____

    9.   _____

    10.   _____

IV.   Fulfilling Professional Roles and Responsibilities

    11.   _____

    12.   _____

    13.   _____

**Appendix I
Tips and Study Aids**

Worksheet 2
Competency Key Titles

List the Key Title for each Competency: (Study them on the Competency study pages, the Competency Chart, and on the PowerPoint® study module, and then write them from memory here.)

I.   Designing Instruction and Assessment to Promote Student Learning

    1. _____

    2. _____

    3. _____

    4. _____

II. Creating a Positive, Productive Classroom Environment

    5. _____

    6. _____

III. Implementing Effective, Responsive Instruction and Assessment

    7. _____

    8. _____

    9. _____

    10. _____

IV. Fulfilling Professional Roles and Responsibilities

    11. _____

    12. _____

    13. _____

Appendix I
Tips and Study Aids

Worksheet 3
Competency Definitions

State each Competency definition in your own words. Use conversational language, like "When I am teaching, I..." You might even want to memorize these definitions in your wording instead of the SBEC definitions. You can use simpler wording, use additional words, etc. NOTE: Personalizing these definitions will help you understand them.

1. _____
   _____
   _____

2. _____
   _____
   _____

3. _____
   _____
   _____

4. _____
   _____
   _____

5. _____
   _____
   _____

6. _____
   _____
   _____

7. _____
   _____
   _____

8. _____
   _____
   _____

9. _____
   _____

10. _____
    _____

11. _____
    _____

12. _____
    _____

13. _____
    _____

Worksheet 4
Key Descriptors

See the Descriptor exercise on p. 10. Use this worksheet to record all of your Descriptor phrases from each Competency chapter in one spot. Suggestion: Place this completed worksheet beside the SBEC study material in the back of this book. Read your Descriptor phrase, try to recall any detailed information you left out, and then check your recall by looking at the SBEC bullet point. It is helpful to number your phrases and the SBEC bullet points. Copy this worksheet when complete and carry it with you for additional study on the go.

Competency 1

_____

_____

_____

_____

_____

_____

_____

_____

_____

_____

_____

_____

_____

_____

Competency 2

_____

_____

_____

_____

_____

_____

_____

_____

_____

_____

_____

_____

_____

Competency 3

_____

_____

_____

_____

_____

_____

_____

_____

_____

_____

_____

_____

_____

Competency 4

_____

_____

_____

_____

_____

_____

_____

_____

_____

_____

_____

_____

Competency 5

_____

_____

_____

_____

_____

_____

_____

_____

_____

_____

_____

_____

_____

_____

Competency 6

_____

_____

_____

_____

_____

_____

_____

_____

_____

_____

_____

Worksheet 4
Key Descriptors, cont'd.

Competency 7

_____

Competency 8

Competency 10

_____

Competency 11

Competency 12

_____

Competency 13

Worksheet 5
Study Assignments

1. **RECALL THE INFORMATION:**

   "Know what you know, and know what you don't know."

   Once during your study time, take blank pieces of paper and write down everything you know about the Competencies. You could include:

   a)   Key Titles

   b)   Competency Definitions

   c)   Detailed information you can recall about each Competency

2. **REWRITE THE QUESTIONS:**

   This is a one-time assignment: **Re-write 3 questions in your own words.** While on the test you might find yourself becoming fatigued and may start rereading questions. This is quite common as some questions are difficult to understand when you read them at first, and even more difficult when you are fatigued. Rewriting the question out to the side in your own words helps you understand the question. In doing this you are using "analysis and synthesis".

3. **PRACTICE TESTS:**

   There are practice test questions in the Study Manual from NES/SBEC and a sampling of those are in the back of this manual. See the "Practice Test Method" in Appendix I of this manual for complete instructions on answering practice questions. Make several copies of the "Practice Test Worksheet" in Appendix III and use it for a practice test answer sheet for any questions you might have access to through your alternative certification program, university, or school district or from other publishers' TExES books. The most important step on this worksheet in Appendix III is the last step...it asks you why the test writers chose the answer that they did. This is a critical step in the process of aligning your thoughts and behavior with the SBEC point of view...what the test is based on.

4. **ANALYZE STRENGTHS AND WEAKNESSES:**

   Review which Competencies you are the weakest in from the activities above. Do extra study on those areas. (Remember, correct reasons for choosing answers is KEY...simply picking the answer for wrong reasons will not help you on the REAL test.)

   GOOD LUCK!

Appendix II

Resources and References

References

Baxter-Magolda, M.B. (1992). *Knowing and Reasoning in College: Gender-related patterns in student's intellectual development.* San Francisco: Jossey Bass.

Barlow, D. L. (1985). *Educational Psychology, the Teaching-learning Process.* Chicago: Moody Press.

Bloom, B. (1976). *Human Characteristics and School Learning.* New York: McGraw-Hill.

Bloom, B. et al. (1956) *Taxonomy of Educational Objectives:* Handbook I, Cognitive Domain. New York: Longmans Green.

Canfield, A.A. & Canfield, J.S. (1988). *Instructional Styles Inventory.* Los Angeles: Western Psychological Services.

Coles, R. (1993). Point of view: When earnest volunteers are soley tested. *Chronicle of Higher Education*, May 5, A52.

Dunn, R., & Dunn, K. (1993). Presentation on Using Learning Styles Information to Enhance Teaching Effectiveness at Learning Styles Institute, Lubbock, Texas, June 5-9. (Sponsored by Education Service Center, Region XVII.)

Elkind, D. (1967). Egocentrism in adolescence. Child Development, 38, 1025-34.

Flavell, J.H. (1979). Metacognition and cognitive monitoring: A new era of cognitive developmental inquiry. *American Psychologist*, 34, 906-911.

Flavell, J.H. (1987). Speculations about the nature and development of metacognition. In R.H. Kluwe & F.E. Weinerrt (Eds.), *metacognition, motivation, and learning* (pp.21-30). Hillsdale, NJ: Erlbaum.

Gagné, R.M. (1977). *The Conditions of Learning,* 3rd Edition. New York: Holt, Rinehart, and Winston.

Lindgren, H.C., Suter, W.N. (1985). *Educational Psychology in the Classroom.* Monterey, CA: Brooks/Cole Publishing

Maslow, A. (1968). *Toward a Psychology of Being.* New York: Van Nostrand Reinhold.

Nolting, P. (1993). Presentation on Meeting Learners' Special Needs at West Texas Regional TASP Workshop, Lubbock, Texas, August 7. (Sponsored by Texas Tech University.)

References, cont'd.

Percival, F. and Ellington H. (1988). *A Handbook of Educational Technology.* London: Kogan Page Limited.

Piaget, J. (1950). *The Psychology of Intelligence.* London: Routledge and Kegan Paul.

Sadker, M., & Sadker, D. (1994). *Failing at Fairness: How America's schools cheat girls.* New York: Charles Scribner's Sons.

Slavin, R.E. (1986). *Using Student Team Learning.* Baltimore: Johns Hopkins University Press.

Slavin, R.E. (1987). "Cooperative Learning and the Cooperative School." *Educational Leadership*, 45:3 (November), pp. 7-13.

Sternberg, R.J. (1985). *Beyond IQ: A Triarchic Theory of Human Intelligence.* Cambridge: Cambridge University Press.

R.E.A. (1998). *The Best Test Preparation for the ExCET.* Piscataway, NJ: Research and Education Association.

Tavris, C. (1994). Presentation on Coping with Student Conflicts Inside and Outside the Classroom at Texas Junior College Teachers Conferences, San Antonio, February 25.

Woodward, P. (1996). *The Teacher's Almanac.* Los Angeles, CA: Lowell House.

ETS (National Evaulation Systems, Inc.) and SBEC (State Board for Educator Standards (Texas)), (2002) TExES Preparation Manuals for EC-4, 4-8, 8-12 and EC-12.

Appendix II
Resources and References

NOTE: The NES/SBEC recommends several books and journals in the back of the NES/SBEC study manual.

TExES Study Materials and Information

TExES Exam Contact Information:

For questions concerning all aspects of the TExES exams, including obtaining TExES Preparation Manuals, test dates, registration deadlines, admission, and scores contact:

• • • • • • ••••••••• •• • •Contact Info for TExES Testing:

www.tx.nesinc.com••

1-800-877-4599

The State Board of Educator Certification contact Information:

SBEC Office of Accountability

SBECPublicComment@tea.texas.gov

www.tea.texas.gov

512-936-8400

Additional Study Resources:

(NOTE: Several preparation resources are listed in the back of the NES/SBEC TExES manual.)

• Additional books for various TExES exams on Amazon.com and in bookstores.

Contacts:

•   Texas Education Agency

1701 North Congress Ave., Austin, TX 78701-1494

888-863-5880

www.tea.texas.gov

•   Texas State Teachers Association

316 West 12th Street, Austin, TX 78701

1-877-ASK-TSTA or 512-476-5355

www.tsta.org

TExES Study Materials and Information, cont'd.

- Secretary of State's Office: www.sos.state.tx.us

- Texas Center for Education Technology:
  www.tcet.unt.edu/home
  e-mail: tcetinfo@www.tcet.unt.edu

- TeachersNet: http://www.teachers.net

- The Association of Texas Professional Educators: http://www.atpe.org

- Texas Classroom Teachers Association: http://www.tcta.org

- Dept. of Education in Washington D.C.: http://www.ed.gov

- Pass the TExES Book and Seminar Program from Ed Publishing and Consulting
  www.passthetexes.com
  e-mail: edpublishing@passthetexes.com
  888-978-1922

Appendix III

Seminar Packet

Pass the Texes PPR

Seminar Packet

Appendix III
Seminar Packet

Copyright © 2018 Ed Publishing

Copy this chart and carry it with you for easy study.

Competencies

Domain I

1. Human Development

Competency 1:
The teacher understands human development processes and applies this knowledge to plan instruction and ongoing assessment that motivate students and are responsible to their developmental characteristics and needs.

2. Diversity

Competency 2:
The teacher understand student diversity and knows how to plan learning experiences and design assessments that are responsive to differences among students and that promote all students' learning

3. TEKS

Competency 3:
The teacher understands procedures for designing effective and coherent instruction and assessment based on appropriate learning goals and objectives.

4. How Learning Occurs

Competency 4:
The teacher understands learning processes and factors that impact student learning and demonstrates this knowledge by planning effective, engaging instruction and appropriate assessments.

Domain II

5. Environment of Support

Competency 5:
The teacher knows how to establish a classroom climate that fosters learning, equity, and excellence and uses this knowledge to create a physical and emotional environment that is safe and productive.

6. Management Issues

Competency 6:
The teacher understands strategies for creating an organized and productive learning environment and for managing student behavior.

Domain III

7. Communication

Competency 7:
The teacher understands and applies principals and strategies for communicating effectively in varied teaching nd learning contexts.

8. Engaging Instruction

Competency 8:
The teacher provides appropriate instruction that actively engages students in the learning process.

9. Technology

Competency 9:
Th teacher incorporates the effective use of technology to plan, organize, deliver, and evaluate instruction for all students.

10. Assessment

Competency 10:
The teacher monitors student per formance and achievement; provides students with timely , high-quality feedback; and responds flexibly to promote learning for all students.

Domain IV

11. Family

Competency 11:
The teacher understands the importance of family involvement in children's education and knows how to interact and communicate effectively with families.

12. Practitioner

Competency 12:
The teacher enhances professional knowledge and skills by effectively interacting with other members of the educational community and participating in various types of professional activities.

13. Texas Teachers

Competency 13:
The teacher understands and adheres to legal and ethical requirements for educators and is knowledgeable of the structure of education in Texas.

Worksheet 1
Competency Key Titles

List the first letter of each Key Title for each Competency: (Study them on the Competency study pages in this manual and on the module, and then write them from memory here.)

I.   Designing Instruction and Assessment to Promote Student Learning

    1. _____

    2. _____

    3. _____

    4. _____

II.   Creating a Positive, Productive Classroom Environment

    5. _____

    6. _____

III.   Implementing Effective, Responsive Instruction and Assessment

    7. _____

    8. _____

    9. _____

    10. _____

IV.   Fulfilling Professional Roles and Responsibilities

    11. _____

    12. _____

    13. _____

Worksheet 2
Competency Key Titles

List the Key Title for each Competency: (Study them on the Competency study pages in this manual and on the module, and then write them from memory here.)

I. Designing Instruction and Assessment to Promote Student Learning

    1. _____

    2. _____

    3. _____

    4. _____

II. Creating a Positive, Productive Classroom Environment

    5. _____

    6. _____

III. Implementing Effective, Responsive Instruction and Assessment

    7. _____

    8. _____

    9. _____

    10. _____

IV. Fulfilling Professional Roles and Responsibilities

    11. _____

    12. _____

    13. _____

Worksheet 3
Competency Definitions

State each Competency definition in your own words. Use a conversational style, like "When I am teaching, I should..." Personalizing these definitions is helpful to your understanding of them. You might want to study these definitions instead of the official ones.

1. _____

_____

2. _____

_____

3. _____

_____

4. _____

_____

5. _____

_____

6. _____

_____

7. _____

_____

8. _____

_____

9. _____

_____

10. _____

_____

11. _____

_____

12. _____

_____

13. _____

_____

Appendix III
Seminar Packet

Worksheet 4
Key Descriptors

See the Descriptor exercise on p. 10. Use this worksheet to record all of your Descriptor phrases from each Competency chapter in one spot. Suggestion: Place this completed worksheet beside the SBEC study material in the back of this book. Read your Descriptor phrase, try to recall any detailed information you left out, and then check your recall by looking at the SBEC bullet point. It is helpful to number your phrases and the SBEC bullet points. Copy this worksheet when complete and carry it with you for additional study on the go.

Competency 1

_____

_____

_____   Competency 3

_____   _____

_____   _____   Competency 5

_____   _____   _____

_____   _____   _____

_____   _____   _____

_____   _____   _____

_____   _____   _____

_____   _____   _____

_____   _____   _____

_____   _____   _____

_____   _____   _____

_____   _____   _____

Competency 2   _____   _____

_____   Competency 4   _____

_____   _____   Competency 6

_____   _____   _____

_____   _____   _____

_____   _____   _____

_____   _____   _____

_____   _____   _____

_____   _____   _____

_____   _____   _____

Worksheet 4
Key Descriptors, cont'd.

_____

_____

_____

_____

_____

_____

Competency 7

_____

_____

_____

_____

_____

_____

_____

_____

_____

_____

_____

_____

_____

_____

_____

_____

_____

_____

Competency 8

_____

_____

_____

_____

_____

_____

_____

_____

_____

_____

_____

_____

_____

_____

_____

_____

Competency 10

_____

_____

_____

_____

_____

_____

_____

_____

_____

_____

_____

_____

_____

_____

_____

Competency 11

_____

_____

_____

_____

_____

_____

_____

_____

_____

_____

_____

_____

_____

_____

Competency 12

_____

_____

_____

_____

_____

_____

_____

_____

_____

_____

_____

Competency 13

_____

_____

_____

_____

_____

_____

_____

_____

_____

_____

_____

_____

_____

Appendix III
Seminar Packet

Worksheet 5
Study Assignments

1. **RECALL THE INFORMATION:**

   "Know what you know, and know what you don't know."

   A few times during your study, take blank pieces of paper and write down everything you know about the Competencies. You could include:

   a) Key Titles

   b) Competency Definitions

   c) Detailed information you can recall about each Competency

2. **REWRITE THE QUESTIONS:**

   This is a one-time assignment: **Re-write 3 questions in your own words.** While on the test you might find yourself becoming fatigued and may start rereading questions. This is quite common as some questions are difficult to understand when you read them at first, and even more difficult when you are fatigued. Rewriting the question out to the side in your own words helps you understand the question. In doing this you are using "analysis and synthesis".

3. **PRACTICE TESTS:**

   There are practice test questions in the Study Manual from NES/SBEC and a sampling of those are in the back of this manual. See the "Practice Test Method" in Appendix I of this manual for complete instructions on answering practice questions. Make several copies of the "Practice Test Worksheet" in Appendix III and use it for a practice test answer sheet for any questions you might have access to through your alternative certification program, university, or school district or from other publishers' TExES books. The most important step on this worksheet in Appendix III is the last step...it asks you why the test writers chose the answer that they did. This is a critical step in the process of aligning your thoughts and behavior with the SBEC point of view...what the test is based on.

4. **ANALYZE STRENGTHS AND WEAKNESSES:**

   Review which Competencies you are the weakest in from the activities above. Do extra study on those areas. (Remember, correct reasons for choosing answers is KEY...simply picking the answer for wrong reasons will not help you on the REAL test.)

   GOOD LUCK!

PRACTICE TEST WORKSHEET
See a detailed explanation for this worksheet in Appendix I.

1) *Restate the question in your own words if necessary.* _____
_____
_____

2) *Determine what Competency the question is referring to.* _____
3) *State why you think this is the correct Competency.* _____
_____
_____

4) *Based on the competency you chose, state your answer* _____
5) *State why this answer is correct, and why it connects to the Competency you chose.* _____
_____
_____

6) *Look up the co ect Competency and answer in the Answer Key.*

7) *Analysis: Why did the test writers chose the answer they did (whether you were right or wrong)? This analysis helps you understand the SBEC point of view.* _____
_____
_____

• •

1) *Restate the question in your own words if necessary.* _____
_____
_____

2) *Determine what Competency the question is referring to.* _____
3) *State why you think this is the correct Competency.* _____
_____
_____

4) *Based on the competency you chose, state your answer* _____
5) *State why this answer is correct, and why it connects to the Competency you chose.* _____
_____
_____

6) *Look up the correct Competency and answer in the Answer Key.*

7) *Analysis: Why did the test writers chose the answer they did (whether you were right or wrong)? This analysis helps you understand the SBEC point of view.* _____
_____
_____

• •

1) *Restate the question in your own words if necessary.* _____
_____
_____

2) *Determine what Competency the question is referring to.* _____
3) *State why you think this is the correct Competency.* _____
_____
_____

4) *Based on the competency you chose, state your answer* _____
5) *State why this answer is correct, and why it connects to the Competency you chose.* _____
_____
_____

6) *Look up the correct Competency and answer in the Answer Key.*

7) *Analysis: Why did the test writers chose the answer they did (whether you were right or wrong)? This analysis helps you understand the SBEC point of view.* _____
_____
_____

Note: This sampling of the SBEC questions is used for the purpose of illustrating our practice test method of documenting your thought processes while answering the questions. It is important to know why you are making certain choices, as well as do an analysis of the test writer's answers. You may copy the page at left several times, and use it as you answer other questions you might be using from another publishing company, your Education Service Center, ACP, university, school district, or other source.

PRACTICE TEST QUESTIONS

SET 1 BEGINS HERE

Andrew Rivera's fourth-grade class has started a health unit that emphasizes the obligations of individuals and societies to protect the environment. In this unit, the class has been discussing their town's landfill crisis. One day the students return from lunch commenting on the amount of waste they saw in the cafeteria that day and noting that all the garbage generated by the school is contributing to the landfill problem. One student, Kahlil, remarks, "If they'd feed us stuff we like better, maybe there'd be less to throw out." Other students join in, talking about how wasteful it is to serve food that nobody likes and wondering what might be done about the waste.

Once the class settles down, the teacher remarks that students have made some very interesting observations and poses the following questions to the class:

Is the amount of food you saw wasted today typical?

Kahlil has suggested that if the school served lunches that students like, there would be less waste. Do you agree or disagree with Kahlil's suggestion, and why?

What kinds of information could you collect to support your opinions?

1. Mr. Rivera's rephrasing of Kahlil's hypothesis is likely to be most useful for:

A. providing a framework for subsequent student discussion.
B. encouraging student recall of related information.
C. checking students' understanding of Kahlil's original statement.
D. providing students with clues about the answer to the preceding question.

Restate the question in your own words if necessary.

_____

_____

Determine what Competency the question is referring to. _____
State why you think this is the correct Competency.

_____

_____

Based on the competency you chose, state your answer _____
State why this answer is correct, and why it connects to the Competency you chose.

_____

_____

Look up the correct competency and answer in the Answer Key.

Analysis: What is the reason the test writers chose the answer that they did (whether you were right or wrong). This will help you understand the SBEC point of view.

_____

_____

2. The primary role that Mr. Rivera has taken in the instructional process so far has been to:

A. encourage students to generate questions about issues that are meaningful to them.
B. prompt students to assess their own understanding of instructional content.
C. facilitate students' use of higher-order thinking in a real-world context.
D. provide students with information that can serve as a basis for future learning.

Restate the question in your own words if necessary.

_____
_____
_____

Determine what Competency the question is referring to. _____
State why you think this is the correct Competency.

_____
_____
_____

Based on the competency you chose, state your answer _____
State why this answer is correct, and why it connects to the Competency you chose.

_____
_____
_____

Look up the correct competency and answer in the Answer Key.

Analysis: What is the reason the test writers chose the answer that they did (whether you were right or wrong). This will help you understand the SBEC point of view.

_____
_____
_____

As they continue talking about the issue of cafeteria waste, the students decide to try to quantify the amount of food and other waste coming from the school cafeteria over a period of time in order to determine the validity of Kahlil's hypothesis regarding the relationship between student food preferences and cafeteria waste. Mr. Rivera asks the class, "How could we organize this research project?" The class responds enthusiastically, suggesting a variety of possible ways to implement such a project.

Finally, the students decide to split into teams, each of which will take on specific responsibilities during each phase of the project. The data collection phase of the project will mainly focus on quantifying the amount of cafeteria food thrown away each day and interviewing students in other classes to determine whether they liked the meal served that day.

3. What is an important advantage of having students play a key role in the planning process for this project?

A. It facilitates the development of a project plan best suited to address the academic needs of individual students.
B. It provides students with an opportunity to structure their own learning.
C. It offers the teacher an opportunity to explore student preconceptions regarding the research topic.
D. It enhances students' recognition of their own strengths and areas for improvement.

Restate the question in your own words if necessary.

_____
_____
_____

Determine what Competency the question is referring to. _____
State why you think this is the correct Competency.

_____
_____
_____

Based on the competency you chose, state your answer _____
State why this answer is correct, and why it connects to the Competency you chose.

_____
_____
_____

Look up the correct competency and answer in the Answer Key.

Analysis: What is the reason the test writers chose the answer that they did (whether you were right or wrong). This will help you understand the SBEC point of view.

_____
_____
_____

4. Mr. Rivera asks the class to consider the possible effects their study could have on the functioning of the cafeteria. Having students think about this issue is most likely to help them:

A. develop a sense of involvement and responsibility in relation to the larger school community.
B. recognize the need for precision and accuracy in carrying out any research effort.
C. gain an appreciation of their own ability to make decisions effectively.
D. recognize the value of establishing and maintaining standards of behavior within the school environment.

Restate the question in your own words if necessary.

_____
_____
_____

Determine what Competency the question is referring to. _____
State why you think this is the correct Competency.

_____
_____
_____

Based on the competency you chose, state your answer _____
State why this answer is correct, and why it connects to the Competency you chose.

_____
_____
_____

Look up the correct competency and answer in the Answer Key.

Analysis: What is the reason the test writers chose the answer that they did (whether you were right or wrong). This will help you understand the SBEC point of view.

_____
_____

**Appendix III
Seminar Packet**

Following analysis of their data, the students write a letter to school administrators describing their research results and making recommendations for student menu plans that could minimize waste. The class receives the following response to their letter from an administrator.

To the Students in Mr. Rivera's Fourth-Grade Class:

I was very impressed with the proposal that you sent me concerning cafeteria waste. It is evident that you have put a great deal of thought and effort into identifying the problem and seeking a solution. You should be very proud of your work.

Although our district has already signed an agreement for all our food purchases for this school year, and we are not able to ask for any changes in the agreement, your proposal has given us something to think about when we plan next year's menus. We have talked about investigating the situation in some other district schools to see if they have the same problems. I would like very much to visit your class to get more details about how you conducted your study and to ask some questions about your proposal. I will contact Mr. Rivera to set up a time.

I want to thank you for your interest and concern about the cafeteria menus. I hope to see you soon to talk more about this. Please feel free to send along any other ideas you may have about the school's waste problems. These are very important issues that affect all of us.

Sincerely,

Raymond Chase
Director of Purchasing

5.   Writing a letter to school administrators most likely served to promote the development of Mr. Rivera's fourth graders by:

A.   encouraging reflection and self-monitoring in the learning process.
B.   teaching them to recognize and appreciate opposing viewpoints on a controversial issue.
C.   enhancing their ability to apply newly acquired information in familiar contexts.
D.   promoting a sense of social responsibility and initiative.

Restate the question in your own words if necessary.
_____
_____
_____

Determine what Competency the question is referring to. _____
State why you think this is the correct Competency.
_____
_____
_____

Based on the competency you chose, state your answer _____
State why this answer is correct, and why it connects to the Competency you chose.
_____
_____
_____

Look up the correct competency and answer in the Answer Key.

Analysis: What is the reason the test writers chose the answer that they did (whether you were right or wrong). This will help you understand the SBEC point of view.

_____
_____
_____

6. Mr. Rivera could best use Mr. Chase's letter in his classroom to achieve which of the following purposes?

A. encouraging students to value careful research by pointing out how research on the school's purchasing system might have led them to produce a better proposal

B. motivating students to engage in similar activities in the futur e by showing them that their ideas with regard to the school's menus were heard and taken seriously

C. helping students learn to appreciate diverse perspectives by discussing with them the costs and benefits of their plan as viewed by the administrator

D. fostering students' understanding of democratic processes by pointing out the probable short- and long-term results of their having spoken out publicly about their ideas

Restate the question in your own words if necessary.

_____
_____
_____

Determine what Competency the question is r eferring to. _____
State why you think this is the correct Competency.

_____
_____
_____

Based on the competency you chose, state your answer _____
State why this answer is correct, and why it connects to the Competency y ou chose.

_____
_____
_____

Look up the correct competency and answer in the Answer Key.

Analysis: What is the reason the test writers chose the answer that they did (whether y ou were right or wrong). This will help you understand the SBEC point of view.

_____
_____
_____

SET 1 ENDS HERE

SET 2 BEGINS HERE

Teresa Foster is a first-year high school social studies teacher. A few weeks into the school year, another social studies teacher, conversing casually with Ms. Foster, remarks, "I hear you have Mary Jordan this year. You must love having her in your class. She was in my class last year, and it was a real pleasure. She's so smart and motivated!"

This remark surprises Ms. Foster because Mary has been one of about a half-dozen students in this particular eleventh-grade class who have seemed especially unmotivated. She has regularly failed to turn in completed homework assignments, has rarely participated in class discussions, and has not done well on quizzes. Ms. Foster had assumed that Mary and the other students had always lacked motivation and had been low achievers. The information from the other teacher prompts Ms. Foster to look into the past academic performance of Mary and the five other students. Her first step is to review their school academic records.

7.   While examining Mary's school file, Ms. Foster observes that Mary's grades have been generally good, with some variation. Mary's social studies grades have been more variable than grades in other subjects. As she interprets these grades, which of the following points should Ms. Foster keep in mind?

A.   Some variation in course grades is normal because different teachers may apply different standards in assigning grades to students.

B.   Seemingly minor fluctuations in course grades over time often indicate severe student stress due to factors outside of school.

C.   Course grades in a given content area tend to be stable because they are based on student work completed over an extended period of time.

D.   Students' grades in a subject area often vary widely over time due to differences in course content from year to year.

Restate the question in your own words if necessary.

_____
_____
_____

Determine what Competency the question is referring to. _____
State why you think this is the correct Competency.

_____
_____
_____

Based on the competency you chose, state your answer _____
State why this answer is correct, and why it connects to the Competency you chose.

_____
_____
_____

Look up the correct competency and answer in the Answer Key.

Analysis: What is the reason the test writers chose the answer that they did (whether you were right or wrong). This will help you understand the SBEC point of view.

_____
_____
_____

As a result of her examination of Mary's school records and conversations with some of Mary's other teachers, Ms. Foster concludes that Mary's school performance was indeed much stronger in previous years. She also discovers that Paul and Leon, two other students in the class, seem to be achieving less during this school year than in the past. Ms. Foster asks Mary, Paul, and Leon to stay after class one day. Following is an excerpt of their discussion.

Ms. Foster: I wanted to talk to you because I've noticed that none of you seem to be doing as well in social studies as I would have expected, given your past performance in school. (The students look down at their desks and say nothing.) You all got A's and B's in social studies last year, but so far, Leon, you're barely passing my class. Mary, with a low C average, you're not doing much better; and Paul, you're doing even worse. I would probably have to give you an F if the grading period were over right now.

(The students shift in their seats but do not say anything.)
Ms. Foster: You all need to start taking steps to improve your performance right away. If you don't, you can't hope to get anything above a C for the term. None of you are turning in homework regularly. Can you tell me why?
Leon: I just don't seem to have enough time to get all of my homework done.
Ms. Foster: Why is that?
Leon: (mumbles) I don't know. (He seems reluctant to say more.)
Ms. Foster: What about you, Mary or Paul? (Both students shrug noncommittally.) All right, you can go now, I guess, but I want you to give some thought to what I've said and we'll talk some more in a day or two.

8. Ms. Foster's handling of this situation is most likely to cause the students to:

A. modify their behavior, but only because of fear of the possible consequences.
B. generalize their negative experience in social studies to other content areas.
C. begin to accept some responsibility for solving problems on their own.
D. feel resentment and mistrust toward the teacher.

* Restate the question in your own words if necessary.
_____
_____
_____

* Determine what Competency the question is referring to. _____
* State why you think this is the correct Competency.
_____
_____

* Based on the competency you chose, state your answer _____
* State why this answer is correct, and why it connects to the Competency you chose.
_____
_____
_____

* Look up the correct competency and answer in the Answer Key.

* Analysis: What is the reason the test writers chose the answer that they did (whether you were right or wrong). This will help you understand the SBEC point of view.
_____
_____
_____

**Appendix III
Seminar Packet**

9. During her meeting with these students, Ms. Foster acted inappropriately by:

A. holding the students to her expectations for their performance rather than their own.
B. suggesting that they would get poor grades for the term if their work did not improve immediately.
C. violating their confidentiality by discussing each one's grades in front of the others.
D. placing too much emphasis on final products and not enough on the learning process.

Restate the question in your own words if necessary.
_____
_____
_____

Determine what Competency the question is referring to. _____
State why you think this is the correct Competency.
_____
_____
_____

Based on the competency you chose, state your answer _____
State why this answer is correct, and why it connects to the Competency you chose.
_____
_____
_____

Look up the correct competency and answer in the Answer Key.

Analysis: What is the reason the test writers chose the answer that they did (whether you were right or wrong). This will help you understand the SBEC point of view.
_____
_____
_____

Since Ms. Foster did not obtain any useful information during the group meeting, she decides to meet with each student individually. When Ms. Foster meets with Mary Jordan, Mary says that she does not have time to do all of her homework because she is working nearly 40 hours a week at two part-time jobs. When Ms. Foster suggests that Mary consider cutting back on the number of hours she devotes to her jobs, Mary becomes agitated. She tells Ms. Foster that her family needs her to work because her mother recently lost her full-time job when the company she worked for went out of business. Ms. Foster next suggests that Mary use her study periods to do her homework, but Mary says she is taking a full class load and has little time to study. Ms. Foster can see that Mary wants to do well in school and is under a great deal of stress.

10. This situation best illustrates which of the following principles?
A. Teachers should be aware that for some students school may serve as a temporary haven from community and family problems.
B. When school and community share information and collaborate to solve problems, the needs of both can be served.
C. Teachers should be aware of family and community problems that may adversely affect students' learning.
D. Students are likely to have less motivation to achieve in school when their basic needs are not being met.

* Restate the question in your own words if necessary.

_____
_____
_____

* Determine what Competency the question is referring to. _____
* State why you think this is the correct Competency.

_____
_____
_____

* Based on the competency you chose, state your answer _____
* State why this answer is correct, and why it connects to the Competency you chose.

_____
_____
_____

* Look up the correct competency and answer in the Answer Key.

* Analysis: What is the reason the test writers chose the answer that they did (whether you were right or wrong). This will help you understand the SBEC point of view.

_____
_____
_____

11. Following her talk with Mary, Ms. Foster receives a phone call from Ms. Jordan, Mary's mother. Ms. Jordan reveals that she is concerned about the effects her problems are having on Mary and admits that she does not know what to do next. It would be most appropriate for Ms. Foster to respond to Ms. Jordan by:

A. asking Ms. Jordan to meet with Mary and her to discuss possible options for balancing Mary's school and job responsibilities.

B. arranging appointments for Ms. Jordan with agencies in the community that can provide family counseling and other family support services.

C. assuring Ms. Jordan that she and other school staff will do whatever they can to modify Mary's instruction to ensure that her schoolwork does not suffer.

D. making an appointment with Ms. Jordan to talk to her about her situation and to offer her advice and support.

* Restate the question in your own words if necessary.

_____
_____
_____

* Determine what Competency the question is referring to. _____
* State why you think this is the correct Competency.

_____
_____
_____

* Based on the competency you chose, state your answer _____
* State why this answer is correct, and why it connects to the Competency you chose.

_____
_____
_____

* Look up the correct competency and answer in the Answer Key.

**Appendix III
Seminar Packet**

Analysis: What is the reason the test writers chose the answer that they did (whether you were right or wrong). This will help you understand the SBEC point of view.

_____

_____

Ms. Foster has discovered that in previous years Paul was a quiet, shy student without many friends. Since the beginning of the current school year, however, Paul's behavior has changed dramatically. He has been associating with a group of students who are unmotivated academically and have reputations as troublemakers. Paul himself has begun acting out in many of his classes. When Paul and Ms. Foster meet, Paul is not very responsive. His answers to her questions are uninformative, and the meeting concludes without resolution. Ms. Foster is concerned because her observations of Paul during class and during her meetings with him convince her that Paul is unhappy and confused; she also suspects that he may be using drugs.

12. Given Ms. Foster's suspicions about Paul's emotional status and possible substance abuse, which of the following would probably be the most effective strategy for her to use first to try to help Paul?

A. discussing with Paul her suspicions regarding his possible substance abuse and the likely consequences of such abuse

B. giving Paul positive reinforcement when he displays desirable behaviors in class and in doing assignments

C. working with appropriate school staff to get Paul into group counseling sessions to identify and address his problems

D. talking to Paul's parents or guardians about her suspicions and strategies they can use at home to modify his behavior

Restate the question in your own words if necessary.

_____

_____

Determine what Competency the question is referring to. _____
State why you think this is the correct Competency.

_____

_____

Based on the competency you chose, state your answer _____
State why this answer is correct, and why it connects to the Competency you chose.

_____

_____

Look up the correct competency and answer in the Answer Key.

Analysis: What is the reason the test writers chose the answer that they did (whether you were right or wrong). This will help you understand the SBEC point of view.

_____

_____

_____

13. Together, Ms. Foster and Leon conclude that one reason for his problems is that he has undertaken too many responsibilities this year (e.g., taking an extra class, working on the school yearbook, beginning a part-time job). Ms. Foster asks Leon to:

* think about his key goals for the year,

* list the various options available to him for dealing with his problem, and

* identify the benefits and costs associated with each option.

Which of the following is a benefit of having Leon carry out this step-by-step process?

A. It models an effective problem-solving strategy that Leon can use in a variety of contexts.

B. It shows Leon how a single problem-solving method can lead to divergent solutions.

C. It encourages Leon to take risks when solving problems on his own.

D. It provides a way for Leon to apply what he has learned in class to solve a real-world problem.

Restate the question in your own words if necessary.

_____
_____
_____

Determine what Competency the question is referring to. _____
State why you think this is the correct Competency.

_____
_____
_____

Based on the competency you chose, state your answer _____
State why this answer is correct, and why it connects to the Competency you chose.

_____
_____
_____

Look up the correct competency and answer in the Answer Key.

Analysis: What is the reason the test writers chose the answer that they did (whether you were right or wrong). This will help you understand the SBEC point of view.

_____
_____
_____

**Appendix III
Seminar Packet**

14. Leon and Ms. Foster further conclude that Leon needs to improve his organizational skills. After they devise a method for keeping track of homework assignments, Ms. Foster suggests that they meet weekly for a few weeks. These steps are likely to benefit Leon most directly by helping him:

A. develop a more positive attitude toward school and toward learning in general.

B. learn how to monitor his own progress and performance more effectively.

C. identify how best to modify activities to suit his individual strengths and needs.

D. become more willing and motivated to participate actively in his learning.

Restate the question in your own words if necessary.

_____
_____
_____

Determine what Competency the question is referring to. _____
State why you think this is the correct Competency.

_____
_____
_____

Based on the competency you chose, state your answer _____
State why this answer is correct, and why it connects to the Competency you chose.

_____
_____
_____

Look up the correct competency and answer in the Answer Key.

Analysis: What is the reason the test writers chose the answer that they did (whether you were right or wrong). This will help you understand the SBEC point of view.

_____
_____
_____

SET 2 ENDS HERE

Not a Set:

15. Joshua is a three-year-old boy who often chooses to play in the block corner during free play time. For several weeks, Joshua's block constructions have consisted primarily of repetitive rows made by placing the blocks end-to end horizontally or by stacking them vertically. Based on this information, the best assessment of Joshua's play with the blocks is that he is:

A. too limited in his approach and needs to be stimulated to explore other types of block construction.

B. passing through a predictable stage in his exploration of the block medium.

C. exhibiting signs of cognitive delay and should be tested for possible cognitive deficits.

D. showing the effects of a home environment in which materials other than blocks are used to provide cognitive stimulation.

Restate the question in your own words if necessary.
_____
_____
_____

Determine what Competency the question is referring to. _____
State why you think this is the correct Competency.
_____
_____
_____

Based on the competency you chose, state your answer _____
State why this answer is correct, and why it connects to the Competency you chose.
_____
_____
_____

Look up the correct competency and answer in the Answer Key.

Analysis: What is the reason the test writers chose the answer that they did (whether you were right or wrong). This will help you understand the SBEC point of view.
_____
_____
_____

16. A preschooler has a pitcher of milk. After pouring milk from the pitcher into three cups, the preschooler announces that she now has more milk. The teacher's best assessment of this incident would be that the student:

A. appears to be showing signs of a developmental delay.

B. has not grasped the concept of conservation of volume.

C. appears to be showing signs of a visual disability.

D. has not developed the concept of object permanence.

Restate the question in your own words if necessary.
_____
_____
_____

Determine what Competency the question is referring to. _____
State why you think this is the correct Competency.
_____
_____
_____

Based on the competency you chose, state your answer _____
State why this answer is correct, and why it connects to the Competency you chose.
_____
_____
_____

Look up the correct competency and answer in the Answer Key.

Analysis: What is the reason the test writers chose the answer that they did (whether you were right or wrong). This will help you understand the SBEC point of view.
_____
_____
_____

17. The students in an eighth-grade class represent a wide range of levels of cognitive development, from concrete operational to formal operational thought. The teacher's best strategy for adapting instruction to accommodate this degree of cognitive variation among student would be to:

A. make use of experiential and hands-on activities to complement and illustrate more abstract content.

B. Group students as much as possible according to level of cognitive development.

C. plan to work with students one-on one to the greatest extent possible.

D. target instruction at the average level of cognitive development represented by the class overall.

Restate the question in your own words if necessary.

_____
_____
_____

Determine what Competency the question is referring to. _____
State why you think this is the correct Competency.

_____
_____
_____

Based on the competency you chose, state your answer _____
State why this answer is correct, and why it connects to the Competency you chose.

_____
_____
_____

Look up the correct competency and answer in the Answer Key.

Analysis: What is the reason the test writers chose the answer that they did (whether you were right or wrong). This will help you understand the SBEC point of view.

_____
_____
_____

18. A high school junior tells a teacher that he intends to drop out of school because school is a waste of time and a full-time job would enable him to earn a lot of money. The teacher is most likely to be able to discuss this issue effectively with the student if the teacher is aware that many students at this age:

A. focus on the present and have trouble appreciating long-term consequences.
B. are not yet able to recognize and distinguish the diverse roles of individuals and groups in society.
C. find it difficult ot apply reasoning skills to any issues that are affecting their own lives.
D. view the authority figures in their lives, including teachers, as being able to make the best decisions.

Restate the question in your own words if necessary.

_____
_____
_____

Determine what Competency the question is referring to. _____
State why you think this is the correct Competency.

_____
_____
_____

Based on the competency you chose, state your answer _____
State why this answer is correct, and why it connects to the Competency you chose.

_____
_____
_____

Look up the correct competency and answer in the Answer Key.

Analysis: What is the reason the test writers chose the answer that they did (whether you were right or wrong). This will help you understand the SBEC point of view.

_____
_____
_____

**Appendix III
Seminar Packet**

ANSWER KEY

Set 1

Item Number	Correct Answer	Competency
1	A	007
2	C	004
3	B	004
4	A	005
5	D	001
6	B	008

Set 2

Item Number	Correct Answer	Competency
7	A	010
8	D	005
9	C	013
10	C	004
11	A	011
12	C	012
13	A	010
14	B	004

Not a set

Item Number	Correct Answer	Competency
15	B	001
16	B	001
17	A	001
18	A	001

NES/SBEC
Competency Study Material

Starting on the next page is the Competency study material for this test from the NES/SBEC manual. The material is directly from the official manual so the page numbers will not corre-spond with the page numbers in our book. We have included this portion of the manual to use with the "Descriptor Exercise" explained in the "Steps for Success" section in the front of this book. The entire manual may be downloaded from the NES/SBEC website, and it is also included with the supplementary files included with this manual.

Domains and Competencies

The content covered by this test is organized into broad areas of content called **domains**. Each domain covers one or more of the educator standards for this field. Within each domain, the content is further defined by a set of **competencies**. Each competency is composed of two major parts:

- The **competency statement**, which broadly defines what an entry-level educator in this field in Texas public schools should know and be able to do.

- The **descriptive statements**, which describe in greater detail the knowledge and skills eligible for testing.

Domain I — Designing Instruction and Assessment to Promote Student Learning

Competency 001: *The teacher understands human developmental processes and applies this knowledge to plan instruction and ongoing assessment that motivate students and are responsive to their developmental characteristics and needs.*

The beginning teacher:

A. Knows the typical stages of cognitive, social, physical and emotional development of students in early childhood through grade 12.

B. Recognizes the wide range of individual developmental differences that characterizes students in early childhood through grade 12 and the implications of this developmental variation for instructional planning.

C. Analyzes ways in which developmental characteristics of students in early childhood through grade 12 impact learning and performance and applies knowledge of students' developmental characteristics and needs to plan effective learning experiences and assessments.

D. Demonstrates an understanding of physical changes that occur in early childhood through adolescence, factors that affect students' physical growth and health (e.g., nutrition, sleep, prenatal exposure to drugs, abuse) and ways in which physical development impacts development in other domains (i.e., cognitive, social, emotional).

E. Recognizes factors affecting the social and emotional development of students in early childhood through adolescence (e.g., lack of affection and attention, parental divorce, homelessness) and knows that students' social and emotional development impacts their development in other domains (i.e., cognitive, physical).

NOTE: After clicking on a link, right click and select "Previous View" to go back to original text.

F. Uses knowledge of cognitive changes in students in early childhood through adolescence (e.g., from an emphasis on concrete thinking to the emergence and refinement of abstract thinking and reasoning, increased ability to engage in reflective thinking, increased focus on the world beyond the school setting) to plan developmentally appropriate instruction and assessment that promote learning and development.

G. Understands that development in any one domain (i.e., cognitive, social, physical, emotional) impacts development in other domains.

H. Recognizes signs of developmental delays or impairments in students in early childhood through grade 4.

I. Knows the stages of play development (i.e., from solitary to cooperative) and the important role of play in young children's learning and development.

J. Uses knowledge of the developmental characteristics and needs of students in early childhood through grade 4 to plan meaningful, integrated and active learning and play experiences that promote the development of the whole child.

K. Recognizes that positive and productive learning environments involve creating a culture of high academic expectations, equity throughout the learning community and developmental responsiveness.

L. Recognizes the importance of helping students in early childhood through grade 12 learn and apply life skills (e.g., decision-making skills, organizational skills, goal-setting skills, self-direction, workplace skills).

M. Knows the rationale for appropriate middle-level education and how middle-level schools are structured to address the characteristics and needs of young adolescents.

N. Recognizes typical challenges for students during later childhood, adolescence and young adulthood (e.g., self-image, physical appearance, eating disorders, feelings of rebelliousness, identity formation, educational and career decisions) and effective ways to help students address these challenges.

O. Understands ways in which student involvement in risky behaviors (e.g., drug and alcohol use, gang involvement) impacts development and learning.

P. Demonstrates knowledge of the importance of peers, peer acceptance and conformity to peer group norms and expectations for adolescents and understands the significance of peer-related issues for teaching and learning.

NOTE: After clicking on a link, right click and select "Previous View" to go back to original text.

Competency 002: *The teacher understands student diversity and knows how to plan learning experiences and design assessments that are responsive to differences among students and that promote all students' learning.*

The beginning teacher:

A. Demonstrates knowledge of students with diverse personal and social characteristics (e.g., those related to ethnicity, gender, language background, exceptionality) and the significance of student diversity for teaching, learning and assessment.

B. Accepts and respects students with diverse backgrounds and needs.

C. Knows how to use diversity in the classroom and the community to enrich all students' learning experiences.

D. Knows strategies for enhancing one's own understanding of students' diverse backgrounds and needs.

E. Knows how to plan and adapt lessons to address students' varied backgrounds, skills, interests and learning needs, including the needs of English-language learners and students with disabilities.

F. Understands cultural and socioeconomic differences (including differential access to technology) and knows how to plan instruction that is responsive to cultural and socioeconomic differences among students.

G. Understands the instructional significance of varied student learning needs and preferences.

H. Knows the ELPS in the domains of listening and speaking in accordance with the proficiency-level descriptors for the beginning, intermediate, advanced and advanced- high levels.

I. Knows the ELPS in the domains of reading and writing in accordance with the proficiency-level descriptors for beginning, intermediate, advanced and advanced- high levels.

Competency 003: *The teacher understands procedures for designing effective and coherent instruction and assessment based on appropriate learning goals and objectives.*

The beginning teacher:

A. Understands the significance of the Texas Essential Knowledge and Skills (TEKS) and of prerequisite knowledge and skills in determining instructional goals and objectives.

NOTE: After clicking on a link, right click and select "Previous View" to go back to original text.

B. Uses appropriate criteria to evaluate the appropriateness of learning goals and objectives (e.g., clarity; relevance; significance; age-appropriateness; ability to be assessed; responsiveness to students' current skills and knowledge, background, needs and interests; alignment with campus and district goals).

C. Uses assessment to analyze students' strengths and needs, evaluate teacher effectiveness and guide instructional planning for individuals and groups.

D. Understands the connection between various components of the Texas statewide assessment program, the TEKS and instruction and analyzes data from state and other assessments using common statistical measures to help identify students' strengths and needs.

E. Demonstrates knowledge of various types of materials and resources (including technological resources and resources outside the school) that may be used to enhance student learning and engagement and evaluates the appropriateness of specific materials and resources for use in particular situations, to address specific purposes and to meet varied student needs.

F. Plans lessons and structures units so that activities progress in a logical sequence and support stated instructional goals.

G. Plans learning experiences that provide students with developmentally appropriate opportunities to explore content from integrated and varied perspectives (e.g., by presenting thematic units that incorporate different disciplines, providing intradisciplinary and interdisciplinary instruction, designing instruction that enables students to work cooperatively, providing multicultural learning experiences, prompting students to consider ideas from multiple viewpoints, encouraging students' application of knowledge and skills to the world beyond the school).

H. Allocates time appropriately within lessons and units, including providing adequate opportunities for students to engage in reflection, self-assessment and closure.

Competency 004: *The teacher understands learning processes and factors that impact student learning and demonstrates this knowledge by planning effective, engaging instruction and appropriate assessments.*

The beginning teacher:

A. Understands the role of learning theory in the instructional process and uses instructional strategies and appropriate technologies to facilitate student learning (e.g., connecting new information and ideas to prior knowledge, making learning meaningful and relevant to students).

B. Understands that young children think concretely and rely primarily on motor and sensory input and direct experience for development of skills and knowledge and uses this understanding to plan effective, developmentally appropriate learning experiences and assessments.

NOTE: After clicking on a link, right click and select "Previous View" to go back to original text.

C. Understands that the middle-level years are a transitional stage in which students may exhibit characteristics of both older and younger children and that these are critical years for developing important skills and attitudes (e.g., working and getting along with others, appreciating diversity, making a commitment to continued schooling).

D. Recognizes how characteristics of students at different developmental levels (e.g., limited attention span and need for physical activity and movement for younger children; importance of peers, search for identity, questioning of values and exploration of long-term career and life goals for older students) impact teaching and learning.

E. Stimulates reflection, critical thinking and inquiry among students (e.g., supports the concept of play as a valid vehicle for young children's learning; provides opportunities for young children to manipulate materials and to test ideas and hypotheses; engages students in structured, hands-on problem-solving activities that are challenging; encourages exploration and risk-taking; creates a learning community that promotes positive contributions, effective communication and the respectful exchange of ideas).

F. Enhances learning for students by providing age-appropriate instruction that encourages the use and refinement of higher-order thinking skills (e.g., prompting students to explore ideas from diverse perspectives; structuring active learning experiences involving cooperative learning, problem solving, open-ended questioning and inquiry; promoting students' development of research skills).

G. Teaches, models and monitors organizational and time-management skills at an age-appropriate level (e.g., establishing regular places for classroom toys and materials for young children, keeping related materials together, using organizational tools, using effective strategies for locating information and organizing information systematically).

H. Teaches, models and monitors age-appropriate study skills (e.g., using graphic organizers, outlining, note-taking, summarizing, test-taking) and structures research projects appropriately (e.g., teaches students the steps in research, establishes checkpoints during research projects, helps students use time-management tools).

I. Analyzes ways in which teacher behaviors (e.g., teacher expectations, student grouping practices, teacher-student interactions) impact student learning and plans instruction and assessment that minimize the effects of negative factors and enhance all students' learning.

J. Analyzes ways in which factors in the home and community (e.g., parent expectations, availability of community resources, community problems) impact student learning and plans instruction and assessment with awareness of social and cultural factors to enhance all students' learning.

K. Understands the importance of self-directed learning and plans instruction and assessment that promote students' motivation and their sense of ownership of and responsibility for their own learning.

NOTE: After clicking on a link, right click and select "Previous View" to go back to original text.

L. Analyzes ways in which various teacher roles (e.g., facilitator, lecturer) and student roles (e.g., active learner, observer, group participant) impact student learning.

M. Incorporates students' different approaches to learning (e.g., auditory, visual, tactile, kinesthetic) into instructional practices.

N. Provides instruction to ensure that students can apply various learning strategies (e.g., using prior knowledge, metacognition, graphic organizers) across content areas, in accordance with the ELPS.

O. Provides instruction in a manner that is linguistically accommodated (communicated, sequenced and scaffolded) to the student's level of English-language proficiency to ensure that the student learns the knowledge and skills across content areas, in accordance with the ELPS.

P. Applies knowledge of the implications for learning and instruction of the range of thinking abilities found among students in any one grade level and students' increasing ability over time to engage in abstract thinking and reasoning.

Domain II — Creating a Positive, Productive Classroom Environment

Competency 005: *The teacher knows how to establish a classroom climate that fosters learning, equity and excellence and uses this knowledge to create a physical and emotional environment that is safe and productive.*

The beginning teacher:

A. Uses knowledge of the unique characteristics and needs of students at different developmental levels to establish a positive, productive classroom environment (e.g., encourages cooperation and sharing among younger students; provides middle-level students with opportunities to collaborate with peers; encourages older students' respect for the community and the people in it).

B. Establishes a classroom climate that emphasizes collaboration and supportive interactions, respect for diversity and individual differences and active engagement in learning by all students.

C. Analyzes ways in which teacher-student interactions and interactions among students impact classroom climate and student learning and development.

D. Presents instruction in ways that communicate the teacher's enthusiasm for learning.

E. Uses a variety of means to convey high expectations for all students.

NOTE: After clicking on a link, right click and select "Previous View" to go back to original text.

F. Knows characteristics of physical spaces that are safe and productive for learning, recognizes the benefits and limitations of various arrangements of furniture in the classroom and applies strategies for organizing the physical environment to ensure physical accessibility and facilitate learning in various instructional contexts.

G. Creates a safe, nurturing and inclusive classroom environment that addresses students' emotional needs and respects students' rights and dignity.

Competency 006: *The teacher understands strategies for creating an organized and productive learning environment and for managing student behavior.*

The beginning teacher:

A. Analyzes the effects of classroom routines and procedures on student learning, and knows how to establish and implement age-appropriate routines and procedures to promote an organized and productive learning environment.

B. Demonstrates an understanding of how young children function in groups and designs group activities that reflect a realistic understanding of the extent of young children's ability to collaborate with others.

C. Organizes and manages group activities that promote students' ability to work together cooperatively and productively, assume responsible roles and develop collaborative skills and individual accountability.

D. Recognizes the importance of creating a schedule for young children that balances restful and active movement activities and that provides large blocks of time for play, projects and learning centers.

E. Schedules activities and manages time in ways that maximize student learning, including using effective procedures to manage transitions; to manage materials, supplies and technology; and to coordinate the performance of noninstructional duties (e.g., taking attendance) with instructional activities.

F. Uses technological tools to perform administrative tasks such as taking attendance, maintaining grade books and facilitating communication.

G. Works with volunteers and paraprofessionals to enhance and enrich instruction and applies procedures for monitoring the performance of volunteers and paraprofessionals in the classroom.

H. Applies theories and techniques related to managing and monitoring student behavior.

I. Demonstrates awareness of appropriate behavior standards and expectations for students at various developmental levels.

NOTE: After clicking on a link, right click and select "Previous View" to go back to original text.

J. Applies effective procedures for managing student behavior and for promoting appropriate behavior and ethical work habits (e.g., academic integrity) in the classroom (e.g., communicating high and realistic behavior expectations, involving students in developing rules and procedures, establishing clear consequences for inappropriate behavior, enforcing behavior standards consistently, encouraging students to monitor their own behavior and to use conflict resolution skills, responding appropriately to various types of behavior).

Domain III — Implementing Effective, Responsive Instruction and Assessment

Competency 007: *The teacher understands and applies principles and strategies for communicating effectively in varied teaching and learning contexts.*

The beginning teacher:

A. Demonstrates clear, accurate communication in the teaching and learning process and uses language that is appropriate to students' ages, interests and backgrounds.

B. Engages in skilled questioning and leads effective student discussions, including using questioning and discussion to engage all students in exploring content; extends students' knowledge; and fosters active student inquiry, higher-order thinking, problem solving and productive, supportive interactions, including appropriate wait time.

C. Communicates directions, explanations and procedures effectively and uses strategies for adjusting communication to enhance student understanding (e.g., by providing examples, simplifying complex ideas, using appropriate communication tools).

D. Practices effective communication techniques and interpersonal skills (including both verbal and nonverbal skills and electronic communication) for meeting specified goals in various contexts.

Competency 008: *The teacher provides appropriate instruction that actively engages students in the learning process.*

The beginning teacher:

A. Employs various instructional techniques (e.g., discussion, inquiry, problem solving) and varies teacher and student roles in the instructional process and provides instruction that promotes intellectual involvement and active student engagement and learning.

NOTE: After clicking on a link, right click and select "Previous View" to go back to original text.

B. Applies various strategies to promote student engagement and learning (e.g., by structuring lessons effectively, using flexible instructional groupings, pacing lessons flexibly in response to student needs, including wait time).

C. Presents content to students in ways that are relevant and meaningful and that link with students' prior knowledge and experience.

D. Applies criteria for evaluating the appropriateness of instructional activities, materials, resources and technologies for students with varied characteristics and needs.

E. Engages in continuous monitoring of instructional effectiveness.

F. Applies knowledge of different types of motivation (i.e., internal, external) and factors affecting student motivation.

G. Employs effective motivational strategies and encourages students' self-motivation.

H. Provides focused, targeted and systematic second language acquisition instruction to English-language learners in grade 3 or higher who are at the beginning or intermediate level of English-language proficiency in listening and/or speaking in accordance with the ELPS.

I. Provides focused, targeted and systematic second language acquisition instruction to English-language learners in grade 3 or higher who are at the beginning or intermediate level of English-language proficiency in reading and/or writing in accordance with the ELPS.

J. Develops the foundation of English language vocabulary, grammar, syntax and mechanics necessary to understand content-based instruction and accelerated learning of English in accordance with the ELPS.

Competency 009: *The teacher incorporates the effective use of technology to plan, organize, deliver and evaluate instruction for all students.*

The beginning teacher:

A. Demonstrates knowledge of basic terms and concepts of current technology (e.g., hardware, software applications and functions, input/output devices, networks).

B. Understands issues related to the appropriate use of technology in society and follows guidelines for the legal and ethical use of technology and digital information (e.g., privacy guidelines, copyright laws, acceptable use policies).

C. Applies procedures for acquiring, analyzing and evaluating electronic information (e.g., locating information on networks, accessing and manipulating information from secondary storage and remote devices, using online help and other documentation, evaluating electronic information for accuracy and validity).

NOTE: After clicking on a link, right click and select "Previous View" to go back to original text.

D. Knows how to use task-appropriate tools and procedures to synthesize knowledge, create and modify solutions and evaluate results to support the work of individuals and groups in problem-solving situations and project-based learning activities (e.g., planning, creating and editing word processing documents, spreadsheet documents and databases; using graphic tools; participating in electronic communities as learner, initiator and contributor; sharing information through online communication).

E. Knows how to use productivity tools to communicate information in various formats (e.g., slide show, multimedia presentation, newsletter) and applies procedures for publishing information in various ways (e.g., printed copy, monitor display, Internet document, video).

F. Knows how to incorporate the effective use of current technology; use technology applications in problem-solving and decision-making situations; implement activities that emphasize collaboration and teamwork; and use developmentally appropriate instructional practices, activities and materials to integrate the Technology Applications TEKS into the curriculum.

G. Knows how to evaluate students' technologically produced products and projects using established criteria related to design, content delivery, audience and relevance to assignment.

H. Identifies and addresses equity issues related to the use of technology.

Competency 010: *The teacher monitors student performance and achievement; provides students with timely, high-quality feedback; and responds flexibly to promote learning for all students.*

The beginning teacher:

A. Demonstrates knowledge of the characteristics, uses, advantages and limitations of various assessment methods and strategies, including technological methods and methods that reflect real-world applications.

B. Creates assessments that are congruent with instructional goals and objectives and communicates assessment criteria and standards to students based on high expectations for learning.

C. Uses appropriate language and formats to provide students with timely, effective feedback that is accurate, constructive, substantive and specific.

D. Knows how to promote students' ability to use feedback and self-assessment to guide and enhance their own learning.

E. Responds flexibly to various situations (e.g., lack of student engagement in an activity, the occurrence of an unanticipated learning opportunity) and adjusts instructional approaches based on ongoing assessment of student performance.

NOTE: After clicking on a link, right click and select "Previous View" to go back to original text.

Domain IV — Fulfilling Professional Roles and Responsibilities

Competency 011: *The teacher understands the importance of family involvement in children's education and knows how to interact and communicate effectively with families.*

The beginning teacher:

A. Applies knowledge of appropriate ways (including electronic communication) to work and communicate effectively with families in various situations.

B. Engages families, parents, guardians and other legal caregivers in various aspects of the educational program.

C. Interacts appropriately with all families, including those that have diverse characteristics, backgrounds and needs.

D. Communicates effectively with families on a regular basis (e.g., to share information about students' progress) and responds to their concerns.

E. Conducts effective conferences with parents, guardians and other legal caregivers.

F. Effectively uses family support resources (e.g., community, interagency) to enhance family involvement in student learning.

Competency 012: *The teacher enhances professional knowledge and skills by effectively interacting with other members of the educational community and participating in various types of professional activities.*

The beginning teacher:

A. Interacts appropriately with other professionals in the school community (e.g., vertical teaming, horizontal teaming, team teaching, mentoring).

B. Maintains supportive, cooperative relationships with professional colleagues and collaborates to support students' learning and to achieve campus and district goals.

C. Knows the roles and responsibilities of specialists and other professionals at the building and district levels (e.g., department chairperson, principal, board of trustees, curriculum coordinator, technology coordinator, special education professional).

D. Understands the value of participating in school activities and contributes to school and district (e.g., by participating in decision making and problem solving, sharing ideas and expertise, serving on committees, volunteering to participate in events and projects).

E. Uses resources and support systems effectively (e.g., mentors, service centers, state initiatives, universities) to address professional development needs.

NOTE: After clicking on a link, right click and select "Previous View" to go back to original text.

F. Recognizes characteristics, goals and procedures associated with teacher appraisal and uses appraisal results to improve teaching skills.

G. Works productively with supervisors, mentors and other colleagues to address issues and to enhance professional knowledge and skills.

H. Understands and uses professional development resources (e.g., mentors and other support systems, conferences, online resources, workshops, journals, professional associations, coursework) to enhance knowledge, pedagogical skills and technological expertise.

I. Engages in reflection and self-assessment to identify strengths, challenges and potential problems; improve teaching performance; and achieve professional goals.

Competency 013: *The teacher understands and adheres to legal and ethical requirements for educators and is knowledgeable of the structure of education in Texas.*

The beginning teacher:

A. Knows legal requirements for educators (e.g., those related to special education, students' and families' rights, student discipline, equity, child abuse) and adheres to legal guidelines in education-related situations.

B. Knows and adheres to legal and ethical requirements regarding the use of educational resources and technologies (e.g., copyright, Fair Use, data security, privacy, acceptable use policies).

C. Applies knowledge of ethical guidelines for educators in Texas (e.g., those related to confidentiality, interactions with students and others in the school community), including policies and procedures described in the Code of Ethics and Standard Practices for Texas Educators.

D. Follows procedures and requirements for maintaining accurate student records.

E. Understands the importance of and adheres to required procedures for administering state- and district-mandated assessments.

F. Uses knowledge of the structure of the state education system, including relationships among campus, local and state components, to seek information and assistance.

G. Advocates for students and for the profession in various situations.

NOTE: After clicking on a link, right click and select "Previous View" to go back to original text.

Pass the TEXES Test Prep Program
Directions for Using the Study Module

Our interactive PowerPoint® study module will help you understand and internalize the Competency framework. See directions below regarding opening and using this module (in the supplementary file download).

NOTE: The files are locked to protect the copyrighted contents. You may get a message about "read-only." Simply click "OK." ALSO, IF YOU WANT TO STOP THE MODULE AT ANY POINT PRESS THE "ESC" KEY ON YOUR KEYBOARD. ENJOY THE MODULE!

PC USERS

A. If you have PowerPoint® follow these directions:
1. Double click on the file "TExES PPR Show.pps " or "TExES PPR Module.ppt".
2. You may get a message stating that you are opening a Macintosh file and the file will be translated. Click "OK."
3. Your module will then open and you must click your mouse to advance to the following page. If the module does not open in the "Show" mode, go under the menu title "Slide Show" and choose "View Show" mode. It is set up for manual advancing but may give you a choice—manual advancing is the mode you want. Once the show starts you are on your way! Follow the directions in the yellow box on each slide.

B. If you do not have PowerPoint® or if you cannot open the file, follow these directions:
1. Go to https://office.live.com/start/PowerPoint.aspx.
2. The application will open and will ask you for the PowerPoint file you want to open.
3. Choose the "TExES PPR Show" or the "TExES PPR Module.ppt" and the module will open. (If you do not see the list of files in the window go to "File Name" and type in "TExES PPR Show" or "TExES PPR Module"). Your module will then open and you must click your mouse to advance to the following page. If the module does not open in the "show" mode and fill your screen, go under the menu title "Slide Show" and choose "View" mode. It is set up for manual advancing but may give you a choice—manual advancing is the mode you want. Once the show starts you are on your way! Follow the directions in the yellow box on each slide.

MAC USERS

A. If you have PowerPoint® on the Mac follow these directions:
1. Launch PowerPoint and open the document "TExES PPR Show.pps" or "TExES PPR Module.ppt".
2. The module will then open and you must click your mouse to advance to the following page. If it does not open up as a "show" and fill your screen go under the "Slide Show" menu heading and choose "View Show" mode. It is set up for manual advancing but in case it gives you a choice, that is what you want. You will be clicking your mouse to advance to each slide. Once the show starts you are on your way! Follow the directions in the yellow box on each slide.

B. If you do not have PowerPoint® or have an older version follow these directions:
1. Go to https://office.live.com/start/PowerPoint.aspx or Google Slides at https://www.google.com/slides/about/ to open the module.
2. A window comes up and asks you for the PowerPoint® file you want to open.
3. Choose the "TExES PPR Show.pps" or "TExES PPR Module.ppt" and choose "show" and the module will open. You must click your mouse to advance to the following page. If it does not open up as a "show" and fill your screen go under the "Slide Show" menu heading and choose "View Show" mode. It is set up for manual advancing but in case it gives you a choice, that is what you want. You will be clicking your mouse to advance to each slide. Once the show starts you are on your way! Follow the directions in the yellow box on each slide.

Please contact 888-978-1922 or e-mail us at edpublishing@passthetexes.com should you have any problems with the module.

10/18